CORINNE TOUATI COHE
NICOLE NEMNI-N

Anglais

Entraînement

Classe de 6ᵉ

Présentation

Pour les parents

Ce cahier **Chouette** couvre en 23 unités les points essentiels du **programme de 6°** en anglais. Il servira **pendant l'année scolaire** pour compléter le travail en classe, et aussi **en vacances** pour bien préparer la rentrée.

Figurent dans chaque unité :
- un rappel des **règles de base** et des **exemples simples** pour réviser,
- un **entraînement systématique** grâce à plus de cent exercices diversifiés centrés sur tous les points importants,
- la rubrique **Mr Thinkalot** pour vérifier qu'on a bien compris.

S'y trouvent aussi de nombreux **jeux**, placés en fin d'unité, un **tableau de verbes irréguliers** et un **index** (p. 87).

Tous les exercices sont corrigés. Ces corrigés sont regroupés dans les **pages centrales** du cahier qui sont **détachables**.

Pour l'élève

Ne va pas trop vite. Révise soigneusement chaque règle avant de faire l'exercice et prends le temps de bien comprendre le corrigé.

Conception : Graphismes
Mise en page : QuoMedia
Dessins : Christian Goux
Logo de Mr Thinkalot : François Dimberton

© HATIER PARIS 1996 - ISBN 2-218-72178-3

Toute représentation, traduction, adaptation ou reproduction même partielle, par tous procédés, en tous pays, faite sans autorisation préalable est illicite et exposerait le contrevenant à des poursuites judiciaires. Réf. : loi du 11 mars 1957, alinéas 2 et 3 de l'article 41. Une représentation ou reproduction sans autorisation de l'éditeur ou du Centre Français d'exploitation du droit de Copie (20, rue des Grands-Augustins 75006 Paris) constituerait une contrefaçon sanctionnée par les articles 425 et suivants du Code pénal.

Sommaire

UNITÉ 1
Le nom 4

UNITÉ 2
L'article 8

UNITÉ 3
L'adjectif qualificatif 11

UNITÉ 4
La comparaison 14

UNITÉ 5
Les pronoms personnels 18

UNITÉ 6
La possession 21

UNITÉ 7
This / That 26

UNITÉ 8
Les mots interrogatifs 28

UNITÉ 9
Les adverbes 32

UNITÉ 10
Quelques indéfinis de quantité 35

UNITÉ 11
Les prépositions 38

UNITÉ 12
Le présent de be 42

UNITÉ 13
There is / There are 47

UNITÉ 14
Have got 50

UNITÉ 15
Can, can't, must, mustn't 54

UNITÉ 16
Les phrases réduites 58

UNITÉ 17
Le présent simple 61

UNITÉ 18
Le présent progressif 66

UNITÉ 19
Le prétérit simple 71

UNITÉ 20
L'expression du futur 75

UNITÉ 21
Les phrases impératives 78

UNITÉ 22
L'heure 80

UNITÉ 23
Les nombres et la date 82

VERBES IRRÉGULIERS 86
INDEX 87
CORRIGÉS (pages centrales)

UNITÉ 1
Le nom

Le nom est un mot qui désigne une personne, un animal, une chose. En anglais, il y a deux catégories de noms : les dénombrables et les indénombrables.

LES DÉNOMBRABLES ET LES INDÉNOMBRABLES

- **Les dénombrables** = ce que l'on peut compter. Ils peuvent se mettre au pluriel.
  - a girl → girl**s**   a cat → cat**s**

- **Les indénombrables** = ce que l'on ne peut pas compter. Ils ne peuvent pas se mettre au pluriel.
  - bread   milk   water   money

1 **Place les mots suivants dans la bonne colonne :** chair – butter – bread – pen – time – dog – milk – story – shoe – meat – egg – salt.

dénombrables	indénombrables
....	....
....	....
....	....

LE PLURIEL DES DÉNOMBRABLES

- **Pluriel en s**

La plupart des dénombrables prennent un **s**.
Ce **s** peut se prononcer [s] : cat**s** [s], book**s** [s].
Il peut se prononcer [z] : chair**s** [z], door**s** [z].

- **Pluriel en es**

Certains dénombrables forment leur pluriel en **es**. Retiens leur orthographe et leur prononciation.

Mots terminés par **s, x, z, sh, ch**...	Quelques mots terminés par **o**	Mots terminés par une consonne + **y**
bus → bus**es** box → box**es** match → match**es** La terminaison **es** se prononce [iz].	potato → potat**oes** tomato → tomat**oes** mais piano → pian**os**	lady → lad**ies** story → stor**ies** baby → bab**ies** mais day → day**s** car le **y** est précédé d'une voyelle.

2 Mets [iz], [z] ou [s] à côté des noms suivants selon leur prononciation.

1. animals: ....
2. buses: ....
3. cassettes: ....
4. drinks: ....
5. chickens: ....

6. brushes: ....
7. banks: ....
8. exercises: ....
9. hats: ....
10. horses: ....

3 Mets les phrases suivantes au pluriel. Dis combien de noms forment leur pluriel en *es*.

1. The bus is coming.
   ....

2. Where's the blue sock?
   ....

3. The baby isn't sleeping.
   ....

4. Take your umbrella.
   ....

5. Where's the box? Is it on the floor?
   ....

Nombre de noms formant leur pluriel en **es** = ...

- Pluriels irréguliers : il faut bien les retenir.
    man → **men**   woman → **women**   child → **children**   tooth → **teeth**   foot → **feet**
- Cas particuliers
  - **People**   Ne prend jamais de **s** quand il signifie "des gens", "du monde".
            People est un nom pluriel qui se construit avec un verbe au pluriel.
            There **are** a lot of people in the street.
            Il y a beaucoup de monde dans la rue.

  - **Hair**   Est invariable. Il est toujours suivi d'un verbe au singulier.
            My hair **is** long.
            Mes cheveux sont longs.

4 Mets les phrases suivantes au pluriel.

1. The dog isn't in the garden.
   ....

2. Is the child playing?
   ....

3. The postman is bringing a letter.
   ....

4. My brother has got a new racket.
   ....

5. My foot is cold.
   ....

5 Mets les phrases suivantes au singulier.

1. The children aren't in the park.
   ....

2. Look at the men : they're playing football.
   ....

3. His shoes are all black.
   ....

4. Are the women watching T.V.?
   ....

5. The knives are on the table.
   ....

1. Le pluriel des noms peut se prononcer de plusieurs manières.
   ❏ Vrai.   ❏ Faux.

2. Les indénombrables peuvent se mettre au pluriel.
   ❏ Vrai.   ❏ Faux.

3. **People** est un nom pluriel bien qu'il n'ait pas de **s**.
   ❏ Vrai.   ❏ Faux.

ONE or TWO?

Trouve le pluriel des noms donnés. En remettant dans le bon ordre les cases bleues, tu obtiendras un mot qui est toujours au pluriel.

1. POTATO
2. MATCH
3. DRESS
4. ARMCHAIR
5. WOMAN
6. BUS
7. BOX
8. BABY
9. UMBRELLA
10. SANDWICH
11. CHILD
12. POSTMAN
13. MAN

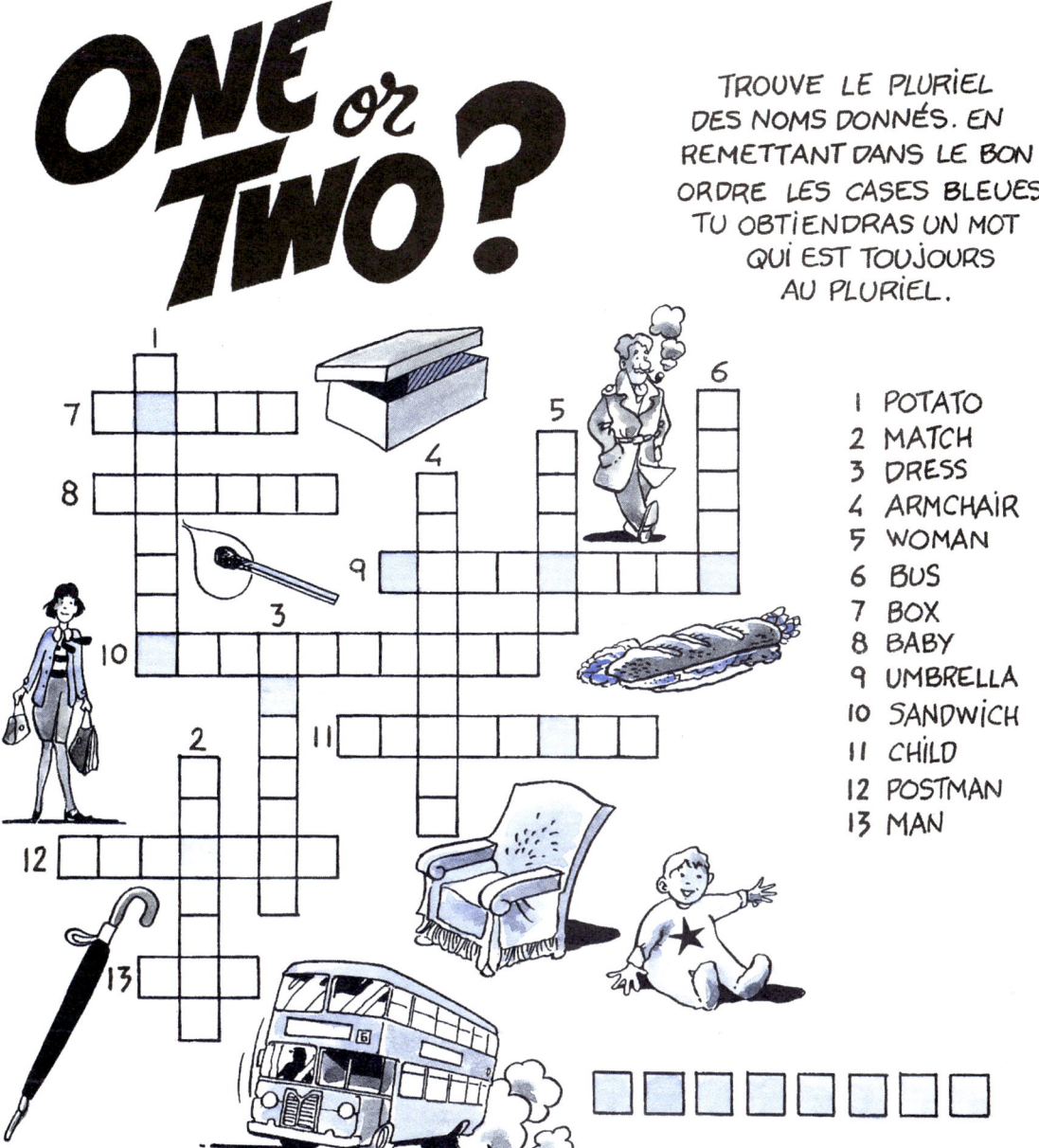

UNITÉ 2
L'article

L'article est un petit mot qui se met devant un nom et qui le détermine. En anglais, il y a deux articles : l'article indéfini (a, an) et l'article défini (the).

A OU THE
Observe bien ces deux dessins.

Take **a** cup.
Prends une tasse.
(n'importe laquelle)

Take **the** cup.
Prends la tasse.
(pas n'importe laquelle, celle qui est sur la table)

A est l'article indéfini. **The** est l'article défini.

L'ARTICLE INDÉFINI : A /AN

- Il existe sous deux formes au singulier :
  - **a** devant une consonne, devant un **y** et un **u** prononcé [ju].
    - **a** ball   **a** cake   **a** year   **a** university
  - **an** devant un mot commençant par une voyelle et un h muet (qu'on ne prononce pas).
    - **an** orange   **an** apple   **an** American man   **an** hour   **an** honest man

- L'article indéfini est le même pour le masculin, le féminin et le neutre.
  - **a** man   **a** woman   **a** chair

- L'article indéfini n'a pas de forme pluriel.
  - There is **a** tree in my garden. *Il y a un arbre dans mon jardin.*
  - There are Ø trees in my garden. *Il y a des arbres dans mon jardin.*

- Il faut employer l'article indéfini devant les noms de métiers au singulier.
  - John is **a** teacher. *John est professeur.*
  - My mother is **an** actress. *Ma mère est actrice.*

---

1 **Complète avec l'article** a **ou** an **ou** Ø **(pas d'article).**

1. My mother is .... teacher.
2. He's coming in half .... hour.
3. He's .... American actor.
4. She's wearing .... yellow dress.
5. There are .... cars in the street.
6. They're .... actors, not .... singers.

2 Construis les questions et les réponses sur le modèle suivant.

Exemple : he / actor / teacher → Is he an actor? No, he isn't. He's a teacher.

1. he / doctor / dentist

....

2. she / actress / nurse

....

3. they / engineers / architects

....

4. he / gardener / policeman

....

5. she / princess / countess

....

L'ARTICLE DÉFINI : THE

• **The** est invariable : il a la même forme au masculin, au féminin et au neutre, au singulier et au pluriel.

the father → **the** fathers   the girl → **the** girls   the car → **the** cars

• **The** se prononce de deux manières :
  • [ðə] devant un nom commençant par une consonne, un **y** ou un **u** prononcé [ju] : **the** [ðə] bus.
  • [ði:] devant un nom commençant par une voyelle : **the** [ði:] orange.

• **The** s'emploie devant les noms déterminés par un complément, par une subordonnée ou par le contexte. **The** ne s'emploie pas dans les généralisations.

    I like **the** cakes she makes. *J'aime les gâteaux qu'elle fait.* (ceux-là)
    I like Ø cakes. *J'aime les gâteaux.* (en général)

On n'emploie pas **the** devant certains noms :
  • Repas : Breakfast is ready. *Le petit déjeuner est prêt.*
  • Langues : I study English. *J'étudie l'anglais.*
  • Activités humaines (jeux, sports, matières scolaires) : I like tennis. *J'aime le tennis.*
  • Jours, mois, saisons : I never work in August. *Je ne travaille jamais en août.*

---

3 Souligne l'article the lorsqu'il se prononce [ði:].

1. the egg
2. the yellow pullover
3. the hat
4. the orange
5. the bus
6. the flower
7. the car
8. the umbrella
9. the tickets
10. the university

4 **Complète avec l'article défini the ou ∅ (pas d'article).**

1. .... blue book is under the table.
2. I often play .... tennis on .... Saturdays.
3. .... dinner is not ready.
4. I like .... English but I don't like .... music.
5. I like .... music of this film.

1. L'article indéfini **a**, **an** sert pour le pluriel.
   ❏ Vrai.   ❏ Faux.
2. **The** se prononce [ði:] devant une voyelle.
   ❏ Vrai.   ❏ Faux.
3. On emploie **the** devant les noms de jours.
   ❏ Vrai.   ❏ Faux.

don't forget!

AJOUTE L'ARTICLE DÉFINI OU L'ARTICLE INDÉFINI (a - an) QUAND CELA EST NÉCESSAIRE, COMME DANS L'EXEMPLE DONNÉ.

BUY **A** PACKET OF CHOCOLATE CAKES
1. BUY .... UMBRELLA.
2. HAVE .... TEA WITH JOHN.
3. BUY JOHN'S .... NEWSPAPER.
4. CALL .... DOCTOR.
5. HAVE .... DINNER WITH OLIVER.
6. BUY .... ENGLISH BOOKS.
7. GO TO TOWN BY .... BUS.
8. CALL MARY ON .... SATURDAY.
9. TENNIS IN .... EVENING.
10. REPAIR .... BIKE.
11. BUY .... PAIR OF SHOES.
12. MEET JIM AT .... WATERLOO STATION.

UNITÉ 3
L'adjectif qualificatif

L'adjectif est un mot qui accompagne le nom et en précise le sens. L'adjectif qualificatif "qualifie" un être, un animal ou une chose, précise ses caractéristiques.

ÉPITHÈTE OU ATTRIBUT

- L'adjectif qualificatif peut être épithète.

    My **new** books are on the table. *Mes nouveaux livres sont sur la table.*

- Il peut être attribut.

    Jane is **beautiful**. *Jane est belle.*

GENRE ET NOMBRE

L'adjectif qualificatif est invariable : il a la même forme au masculin, au féminin, au neutre, au singulier et au pluriel.

My brother is **nice**.   My friends are **nice**.

PLACE

L'adjectif épithète se place avant le nom.

There is a **blue** door in my **new** house.
Il y a une porte bleue dans ma nouvelle maison.
Show me your **yellow** dress.
Montre-moi ta robe jaune.

---

1 Fais une seule phrase à partir des deux phrases données.

Exemple : It's a book. It's red. → It's a red book.

1. It's a car. It's new. → ....
2. It's an armchair. It's comfortable. → ....
3. It's an exercise. It's difficult. → ....
4. It's a pen. It's expensive. → ....
5. It's a house. It's big. → ....

LES ADJECTIFS DE NATIONALITÉ

Ils prennent une majuscule.

Paul is driving an **E**nglish car. *Paul conduit une voiture anglaise.*
Allison is **A**merican. *Allison est américaine.*

LES SUITES D'ADJECTIFS

Si une phrase contient plusieurs adjectifs, l'adjectif de dimension se place avant l'adjectif de couleur.

a **big** black cat: *un gros chat noir*
a **small** orange ball: *une petite balle orange*

2 **Forme des phrases avec les mots fournis dans le désordre.**

1. teacher / her / English / nice / patient / and / is ....
2. her / is / new / this / dress ....
3. young / is / a / she / very / doctor ....
4. wearing / a / dirty / is / he / pullower ....
5. an / this / Italian / is / restaurant / ? ....

3 **Décris les dessins en utilisant les adjectifs donnés :** dirty - big - old - heavy - tall - comfortable.

Exemple : It's a comfortable armchair.

1. It's ....

2. It's ....

3. They're ....

4. They're ....

5. She's ....

4 **Choisis dans la liste le contraire des adjectifs :** bad - long - young - small - cheap.

1. old ≠ ....
2. expensive ≠ ....
3. big ≠ ....
4. short ≠ ....
5. good ≠ ....

1. Les adjectifs de nationalité prennent toujours une majuscule.
   ❏ Vrai.   ❏ Faux.
2. Les adjectifs qualificatifs s'accordent avec le nom qu'ils précisent.
   ❏ Vrai.   ❏ Faux.
3. Quand place-t-on l'adjectif avant le nom ?
   ❏ Quand il est épithète.   ❏ Quand il est attribut.

ON THE CONTRARY

TROUVE LE CONTRAIRE DES ADJECTIFS DONNÉS. INSCRIS-LES DANS LA GRILLE. LA COLONNE BLEUE TE DONNERA LE NOM D'UN PAYS.

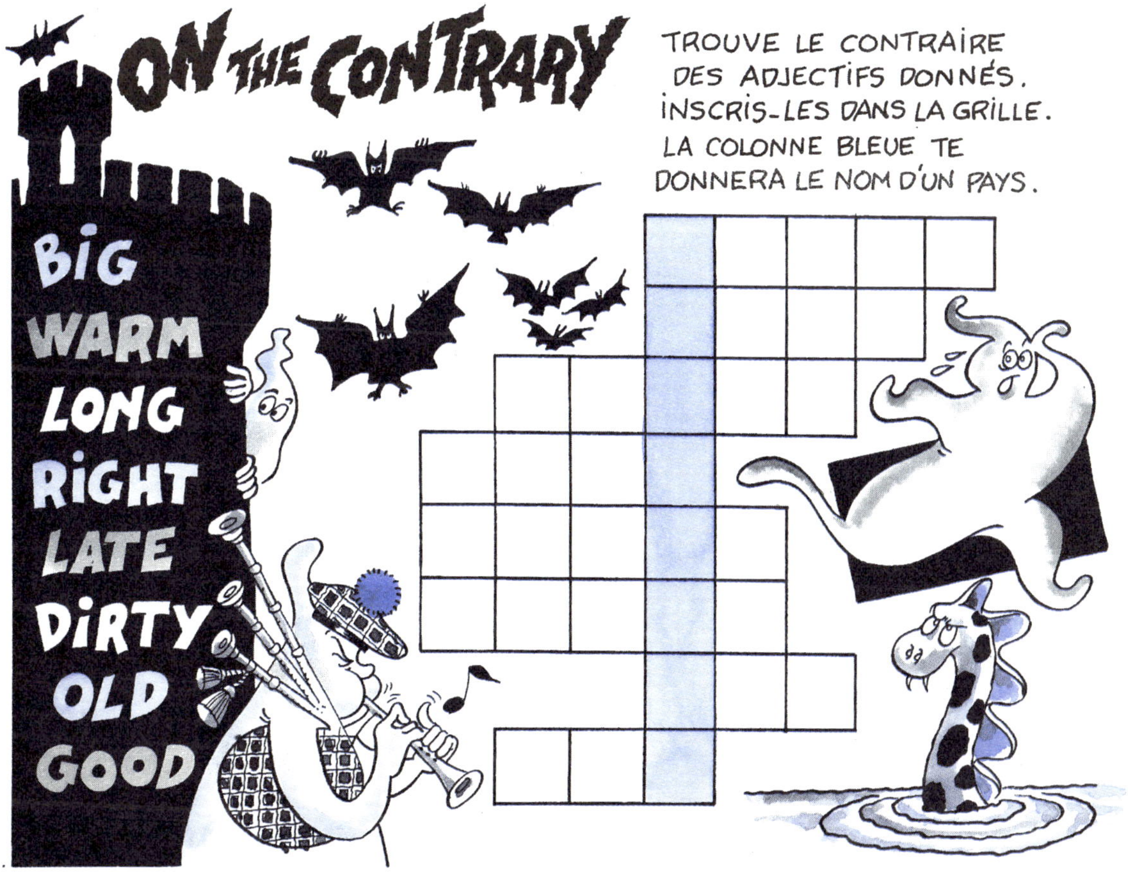

BIG
WARM
LONG
RIGHT
LATE
DIRTY
OLD
GOOD

UNITÉ 4
La comparaison

L'adjectif au comparatif permet de comparer des personnes, des animaux ou des choses.

LE COMPARATIF D'ÉGALITÉ : AS + ADJECTIF + AS

Le comparatif d'égalité se forme en mettant **as** de chaque côté de l'adjectif.

Jimmy is **as** strong **as** Bill. *Jimmy est aussi fort que Bill.*
My tennis racket is **as** expensive **as** your bicycle.
Ma raquette de tennis est aussi chère que ta bicyclette.
Jessica isn't **as** old **as** Ben. *Jessica n'est pas aussi âgée que Ben.*

1 **Construis des phrases avec les éléments donnés.**

Exemple : Mrs Johnson / old / Mrs Robinson → Mrs Johnson is as old as Mrs Robinson.

1. my house / big / Ted's house
   ....

2. her cousin / tall / my brother
   ....

3. Oliver / hungry / Jim
   ....

4. tigers / strong / lions
   ....

5. your shirt / clean / my shirt
   ....

LE COMPARATIF DE SUPÉRIORITÉ

Comparatif des adjectifs courts : adjectif court + **er** + **than**.

Bill is tall**er than** John. *Bill est plus grand que John.*
Your skirt is short**er than** Helen's. *Ta jupe est plus courte que celle d'Helen.*

• Sont considérés comme adjectifs courts, les adjectifs d'une syllabe et les adjectifs de deux syllabes qui se terminent par **y** et **er**.

happy → happ**ier**   clever → clever**er**

• Attention aux changements orthographiques.

big → bi**gg**er   fat → fa**tt**er
hea**v**y → hea**v**ier   funn**y** → funn**ier**

2 Trouve les comparatifs des adjectifs donnés. Les lettres bleues remises dans le bon ordre te donneront le nom d'une spécialité américaine.

1. short → . . . . . .
2. fast → . . . . . .
3. funny → . . . . . .
4. good → . . . . . .
5. easy → . . . . . .
6. happy → . . . . . .
7. clean → . . . . . .
8. cheap → . . . . . .
9. rich → . . . . . .
10. big → . . . . . .
11. heavy → . . . . . .
12. hot → . . . . . .
13. small → . . . . . .

The American speciality is : . . . .

3 Construis des phrases avec les éléments donnés.

Exemple : my brother / tall / John → My brother is taller than John.

1. the chocolate cake / good / the biscuits
   ....
2. Betty / young / Allison
   ....
3. her car / dirty / Peter's car
   ....
4. your bag / heavy / my bag
   ....
5. your hair / long / Jane's
   ....
6. Tom / happy / Bob
   ....
7. the Sahara desert / hot / California
   ....

● Comparatif des adjectifs longs : **more** + adjectif long + **than**.
The armchair is **more** comfortable **than** the chair.
Le fauteuil est plus confortable que la chaise.

4. Construis des phrases avec les éléments donnés.

Exemple : Ben's car / expensive / Michael's → Ben's car is more expensive than Michael's.

1. this armchair / comfortable / this chair
   ....
2. exercise 3 / difficult / exercise 2
   ....
3. this film / interesting / this book
   ....
4. Jessica / polite / Julie
   ....
5. tigers / dangerous / cats
   ....
6. Mrs Bridge / beautiful / Miss Smith
   ....
7. my father / careful / my uncle
   ....

LES COMPARATIFS IRRÉGULIERS
Certains adjectifs ont des comparatifs irréguliers. Il faut bien les retenir.
good → **better**   bad → **worse**

5. Mets les adjectifs entre parenthèses au comparatif de supériorité.

1. My sandwich is .... your pizza. (*good*)
2. Fred's exercise is .... Jane's. (*easy*)
3. Paris is .... Liverpool. (*big*)
4. This restaurant is .... the other one. (*bad*)
5. Mrs Harris is .... Mrs Bridge. (*elegant*)

1. Que met-on de chaque côté de l'adjectif pour former le comparatif d'égalité ?

   ❏ More.   ❏ As.

2. **More** se place devant l'adjectif long pour former le comparatif de l'adjectif long.

   ❏ Vrai.   ❏ Faux.

3. **Better** est le comparatif irrégulier de **bad**.

   ❏ Vrai.   ❏ Faux.

OLDER and HEAVIER

REGARDE LES PERSONNAGES ET RÉPONDS AUX QUESTIONS.

1. WHO IS OLDER THAN JONATHAN? . . . .
2. WHO IS TALLER THAN DAVE? . . . .
3. WHO IS SMALLER THAN JONATHAN? . . . .
4. WHO IS HEAVIER THAN JONATHAN? . . . .
5. WHO IS HEAVIER THAN DAVE? . . . .
6. WHO IS YOUNGER THAN JENNIFER? . . . .
7. WHO IS YOUNGER THAN MARGARET? . . . .

UNITÉ 5
Les pronoms personnels

Les pronoms personnels permettent de remplacer les noms. Ils peuvent être sujets ou compléments.

LES PRONOMS PERSONNELS SUJETS

I
you
he, she, it
we
you
they

He s'emploie pour le masculin. **She** s'emploie pour le féminin. **It** s'emploie généralement pour le neutre (objets, animaux). Mais on emploie **he** ou **she** pour un animal domestique. **You** sert à traduire "tu" et "vous".

1 Remplace les mots *en italique* par le pronom personnel sujet correspondant.

1. *Sally and Bridget* can speak English. ....
2. *His sister* is coming to the party. ....
3. *My cousin Peter* lives in New York. ....
4. *Your parents* are never late. ....
5. *Her brother and I* often go to concerts. ....

LES PRONOMS PERSONNELS COMPLÉMENTS

me
you
him, her, it
us
you
them

Le pronom personnel complément se place toujours après le verbe.
  He loves **her**. *Il l'aime.*
  Do you love **me**? *Est-ce que vous m'aimez ?*
  I must help **them**. *Je dois les aider.*

2 **Choisis le pronom personnel correct.**

1. Listen to (*him - her*). He is singing.
2. These tourists can't speak French. Help (*them - they*).
3. We're late! Take (*us - we*) to the airport.
4. I'm hungry; give (*me - her*) a sandwich.
5. Those chairs are broken; repair (*it - them*).

3 **Remplace par le pronom personnel qui convient.**

1. Look at my mother.
→ Look at ....
2. Where are the children?
→ Where are .... ?
3. He's playing with my sister and I.
→ He's playing with ....
4. What colour is your car?
→ What colour is .... ?
5. Listen to your father.
→ Listen to ....

4 **Forme des phrases à l'aide des mots suivants mis dans le bon ordre.**

1. I / waiting / them / am / for
....
2. he / me / after / is / running
....
3. help / you / us / can / ?
....
4. buy / a / car / they / can't / new
....
5. piece / her / give / a / cake / of
....

1. Où se place le pronom personnel complément ?
   ❑ Avant le verbe.   ❑ Après le verbe.
2. On emploie **you** pour "tu" et "vous".
   ❑ Vrai.   ❑ Faux.
3. On emploie **he** pour le masculin, **she** pour le féminin.
   ❑ Vrai.   ❑ Faux.

The balloons

RETROUVE DANS LA 2ᵉ POIGNÉE DE BALLONS LA RÉPONSE BRÈVE CORRESPONDANT À CHAQUE QUESTION.

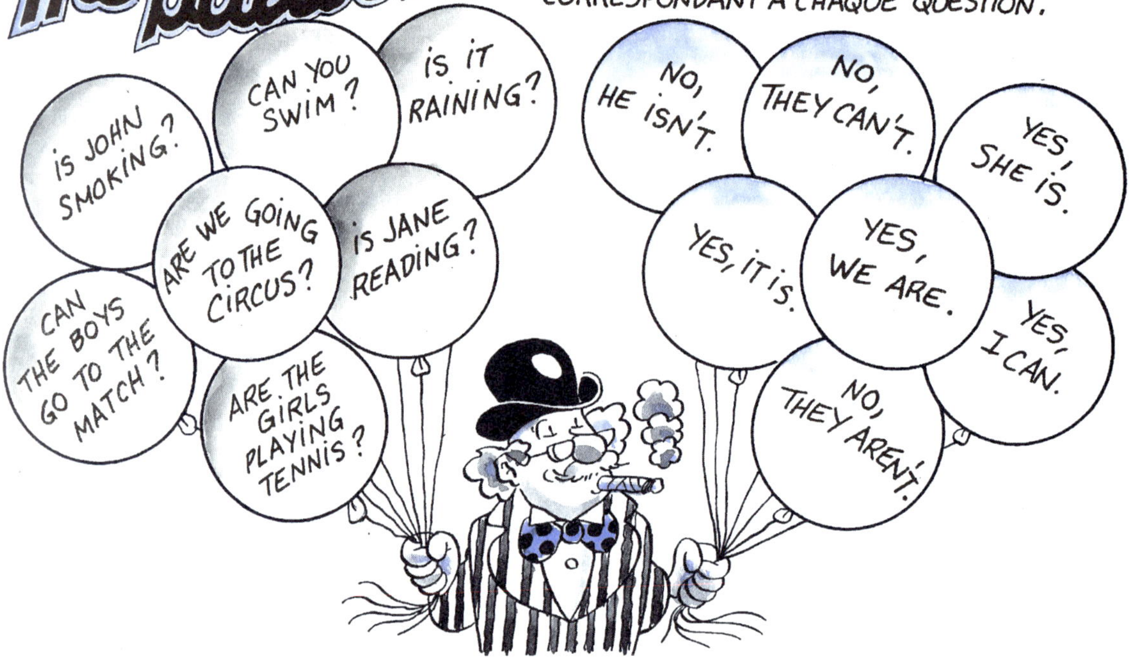

- IS JOHN SMOKING?
- CAN YOU SWIM?
- IS IT RAINING?
- CAN THE BOYS GO TO THE MATCH?
- ARE WE GOING TO THE CIRCUS?
- IS JANE READING?
- ARE THE GIRLS PLAYING TENNIS?

- NO, HE ISN'T.
- NO, THEY CAN'T.
- YES, SHE IS.
- YES, IT IS.
- YES, WE ARE.
- YES, I CAN.
- NO, THEY AREN'T.

UNITÉ 6
La possession

Les relations entre les personnes et l'idée de posséder s'expriment de différentes manières en anglais.

LES DÉTERMINANTS POSSESSIFS

- Voici la liste des déterminants possessifs qu'il faut apprendre par cœur

my ball	**our** ball
your ball	**your** ball
his, her, its ball	**their** ball

- Remarque bien : ils sont toujours suivis d'un nom mais (contrairement au français), ils ne s'accordent pas avec ce nom.

    Look at **my** book! *Regarde mon livre !*
    Look at **my** shoes! *Regarde mes chaussures !*

- Observe bien ces deux dessins.

His name is John.
Look at **his** bike.

Her name is Mary.
Look at **her** bike.

À la 3ᵉ personne du singulier, on choisit **his** (M), **her** (F) ou **its** (N) en fonction du possesseur.

    It's **his** bike. *C'est sa bicyclette (= la bicyclette de John).*
    It's **her** bike. *C'est sa bicyclette (= la bicyclette de Mary).*
    I like **its** colour. *J'aime sa couleur (= la couleur de la bicyclette).*

---

1 Complète à l'aide des déterminants possessifs.

1. It's Mary's bag. It's .... bag.
2. It's Elton's piano. It's .... piano.
3. It's Mr and Mrs Brown's car. It's .... car.
4. Look at the bird's nest. Look at .... nest.
5. It's the children's room. It's .... room.

LE GÉNITIF (CAS POSSESSIF)

- Observe bien.

Oliver's ball
le ballon d'Olivier

le sac de ma mère
my mother's bag

Oliver's et **my mother's** sont des génitifs. Le génitif exprime la possession.
La possession est exprimée au singulier par **'s** suivi d'un nom sans déterminant (**ball, bag**).
Le possesseur (**Oliver, my mother**) est placé en premier.

- Au pluriel, le **s** du cas possessif disparaît, mais l'apostrophe demeure.

    the girl**s'** ball: *le ballon des filles*
    my friend**s'** house: *la maison de mes amis*

Lorsque le pluriel est irrégulier, on emploie **'s**.

    women**'s** clothes: *des vêtements de femmes*
    the **children's** room: *la chambre des enfants*

- Le génitif peut aussi exprimer la relation entre les personnes.

    Here is **my brother's wife**. *Voici la femme de mon frère.*

2. Réponds aux questions comme dans l'exemple donné.

Exemple : Whose bike is it? (*Cathy*) → It's Cathy's bike. It's her bike.

1. Whose pen is it? (*my mother*) ....
2. Whose socks are they? (*Philip*) ....
3. Whose cat is it? (*the Browns*) ....
4. Whose glasses are they? (*Mrs Barret*) ....
5. Whose newspaper is it? (*Allison*) ....

WHOSE?

- **Whose?** sert à interroger sur l'appartenance.

    Whose book is this? It is **John's book**.
    À qui est ce livre ? C'est le livre de John.

- Pour éviter la répétition, on peut répondre par le génitif seul.

    Whose book is this? It's **John's**.

- On peut aussi répondre en utilisant un déterminant possessif suivi d'un nom.

    Whose bag is it? It is **my** bag.
    À qui est ce sac ? C'est mon sac.

3 **Donne une réponse négative et complète.**

Exemple : Is it Julie's bed? (*Betty*) No, it isn't. It's Betty's.

1. Is it Norman's chair? (*John*) ....
2. Is it Jessica's watch? (*Julie*) ....
3. Is it Ben's orange? (*Oliver*) ....
4. Is it my cousin's plate? (*Sam*) ....
5. Is it my brother's pullover? (*my sister*) ....

4 **À partir des deux éléments donnés, reconstitue la question et la réponse correspondante.**

Exemple : Oliver / piano → Whose piano is it? It's Oliver's.

1. my parents / room ....
2. Mr Miller / eggs ....
3. children / rackets ....
4. Diana / dress ....
5. Susan / baby ....

5 **À partir des deux éléments donnés, reconstitue la question et la réponse correspondante.**

Exemple : Jim / cat → Whose cat is this? It's his cat.

1. my friends / bikes ....
2. Maureen / shoes ....
3. Gregory / ball ....
4. Cathy and I / car ....
5. I / breakfast ....

HAVE GOT

Have got sert également à exprimer la possession.
   He **has got** a car. *Il a une voiture.*
   Have they **got** a big dog? Yes, they have.
   Ont-ils un gros chien ? Oui.
Voir aussi p. 50

6 Regarde les dessins et complète les phrases en utilisant have got.

1. He ....

2. She ....

3. They ....

4. He ....

5. She ....

1. **My**, **your**, **his**, **her** déterminants sont toujours suivis d'un nom.
   ❏ Vrai.   ❏ Faux.
2. Quel mot interrogatif sert à interroger sur l'appartenance ?
   ❏ What?   ❏ Whose?
3. Lorsque le possesseur a un pluriel régulier, le **s** du cas possessif disparaît.
   ❏ Vrai.   ❏ Faux.

WHOSE SHOE IS IT?

POSE DES QUESTIONS ET DONNE DES RÉPONSES.

Exemple :
Whose shoe is it ?
It's John's shoe.

UNITÉ 7
This / That

This et that **sont des déterminants du nom. Ils servent à désigner une personne ou un objet. Ce sont des démonstratifs.**

FORMES
This et **that** ont une forme différente au singulier et au pluriel.

this dress: *cette robe* → **these** dresses: *ces robes*
that chair: *cette chaise* → **those** chairs: *ces chaises*

1 Mets les phrases au pluriel.

1. This is my book. → ....
2. That's my pen. → ....
3. This is your ball. → ....
4. That's my racket. → ....
5. This is my shoe. → ....

SENS : PROXIMITÉ / ÉLOIGNEMENT

Look at **this** picture. *Regarde cette image.*   Look at **that** plane. *Regarde cet avion.*

This / these désignent la proximité dans l'espace. Ils peuvent également désigner ce qui est proche de nous, de notre univers.

This chair is comfortable. *Cette chaise est confortable.*
I don't like **that** dog. *Je n'aime pas ce chien. (Je le rejette)*

That / those désignent l'éloignement dans l'espace. Ils peuvent également désigner ce qui est éloigné de nous, de notre univers.

2. Pose la question et donne la réponse. Emploie this ou that selon le sens.

Exemple : What's that? It's a taxi.

1. .... ? ....
2. .... ? ....
3. .... ? ....
4. .... ? ....
5. .... ? ....

3. Mets ces phrases au singulier.

1. Those paintings are expensive. ....
2. These pens are John's. ....
3. Those roses are beautiful. ....
4. These cakes are very good. ....
5. These exercises are easy. ....

1. **That** sert à désigner ce qui est loin de nous.
   ❏ Vrai.   ❏ Faux.
2. **These** est le pluriel de **this**.
   ❏ Vrai.   ❏ Faux.
3. Pour désigner ce qui fait partie de notre univers, il faut utiliser **this**.
   ❏ Vrai.   ❏ Faux.

UNITÉ 8
Les mots interrogatifs

Comme son nom l'indique, le mot interrogatif sert à interroger, à poser des questions.

WH - QUESTIONS

- **What** interroge sur les choses, sur l'action.

  What is it? It's a pen.
  Qu'est-ce que c'est ? C'est un stylo..
  What are you drinking? I'm drinking water.
  Qu'est-ce tu bois ? Je bois de l'eau.
  What colour is your book? It's red.
  De quelle couleur est ton livre ? Il est rouge.
  What is he doing? He is singing.
  Que fait-il ? Il chante.

- **Who** interroge sur l'identité de la personne.

  Who is working today? John is working today.
  Qui travaille aujourd'hui ? John travaille aujourd'hui.

- **Whose** interroge sur l'appartenance.

  Whose car is it? It is Bob's car.
  À qui est cette voiture ? C'est la voiture de Bob.

- **When** interroge sur le temps.

  When do you play tennis? I play tennis on Saturdays.
  Quand joues-tu au tennis ? Je joue au tennis le samedi.

- **Where** interroge sur le lieu.

  Where is he? He is in the park.
  Où est-il ? Il est dans le parc.

- **Why** interroge sur la cause.

  Why is he angry? He is angry because they are late.
  Pourquoi est-il en colère ? Il est en colère parce qu'ils sont en retard.

1 Regarde les réponses et trouve le mot interrogatif manquant.

1. .... are they going? They're going to the country.
2. .... is he coming? Tomorrow.
3. .... is your brother doing? He's working.
4. .... transistor is it? It's Daniel's.
5. .... is it? It's Patrick.

2 Pose des questions portant sur les mots en gras.

1. **Michael**'s in the garden. ....
2. The transistor is **on the table**. ....
3. He's eating **an apple**. ....
4. They're **at the supermarket**. ....

5. It's **Jane**'s racket. ....
6. **John** is coming with her. ....
7. Bill and Ted are going to the circus **on Sunday.** ....
8. He's washing his pullover **because it's dirty.** ....
9. She's sleeping **in an armchair.** ....
10. His umbrella is **blue.** ....

QUESTIONS AVEC HOW

How interroge sur le comment des choses, sur la manière.	**How** do you make this cake? I make this cake with chocolate and nuts. *Comment fais-tu ce gâteau ? Je fais ce gâteau avec du chocolat et des noisettes.*
How old interroge sur l'âge.	**How old** are you? I am sixteen years old. *Quel âge as-tu ? J'ai seize ans.*
How many interroge sur le nombre (suivi d'un pluriel).	**How many** students are there in the classroom? There are ten students in the classroom. *Combien y a-t-il d'étudiants dans la classe ? Il y a dix étudiants dans la classe.*
How much interroge sur la quantité (suivi d'un indénombrable) et sur le prix.	**How much** milk do you want? I want two bottles. *Combien de lait veux-tu ? Je veux deux bouteilles.* **How much** is it? It is 15 dollars. *Combien cela coûte-t-il ? Cela coûte 15 dollars.*

3 Regarde les réponses et trouve le mot interrogatif manquant.

1. .... are you? I am fine, thank you.
2. .... is your sister? She is 15 years old.
3. .... money has he got? He has got a lot of money.
4. .... is this pullover? It's 15 pounds.
5. .... journalists are there at the party? About 20.

4 Pose des questions sur les images en tenant compte des réponses données.

1. ....? It's Tom's.

2. ....? Sally's in her bath.

3. ....? He's washing his car.

4. ....? Ken's five years old.

5. ....? She's going on Saturday.

PLACE DE LA PRÉPOSITION

Si le pronom interrogatif est accompagné d'une préposition, il faut la rejeter en fin de question, après le verbe.

What are you listening **to**? *Qu'est-ce que tu écoutes ?*
Where do you come **from**? *D'où viens-tu ?*
What are you looking **at**? *Que regardes-tu ?*

5 Ajoute la préposition manquante.

1. What are you playing ....? A ball.
2. What are you looking ....? A painting.
3. What are you waiting ....? The bus.
4. Where do you come ....? Italy.
5. What are you listening ....? Dance music.

1. **How much** sert à interroger sur le prix.
   ❏ Vrai.   ❏ Faux.

2. Pour savoir à qui appartient quelque chose, il faut utiliser :
   ❏ What?   ❏ Whose?

3. Où doit-on généralement placer la préposition qui accompagne le mot interrogatif ?
   ❏ À côté du mot interrogatif.   ❏ À la fin de la question.

Cindy's diary

QUE FAIT CINDY CETTE SEMAINE ? À PARTIR DES RÉPONSES DONNÉES, COMPLÈTE LES QUESTIONS.

- MONDAY: buy 2 tickets for the concert
- TUESDAY: dance class: 11. dinner with John at "Fred's"
- WEDNESDAY: dentist at 3.
- THURSDAY: tea with Pamela
- FRIDAY: lunch with Kate concert: 8.30
- SATURDAY: tennis lesson, call Susan
- SUNDAY: picnic
- NOTES: tickets: £28

1. .... IS SHE DOING ON SUNDAY ? SHE'S GOING ON A PICNIC.
2. .... IS SHE HAVING A DANCE CLASS ? ON TUESDAY.
3. .... IS SHE HAVING TEA .... ? PAMELA.
4. .... ARE THE CONCERT TICKETS ? £28.
5. .... IS SHE DOING ON WEDNESDAY ? SHE'S GOING TO THE DENTIST'S.
6. .... IS SHE CALLING ON SATURDAY ? SUSAN.
7. .... IS THE CONCERT ? IT'S AT 8.30.
8. .... IS SHE HAVING DINNER ON TUESDAY ? AT "FRED'S".
9. .... TICKETS MUST SHE BUY ? 2.
10. .... IS SHE HAVING A TENNIS LESSON ? ON SATURDAY.

UNITÉ 9
Les adverbes

L'adverbe est un mot qui accompagne un verbe pour en préciser le sens.

LES ADVERBES EN -LY
Les adverbes se forment généralement en ajoutant **-ly** à l'adjectif.

slow → slow**ly**

Jane speaks quick**ly**. *Jane parle vite.*

Attention !
- Adjectifs terminés par un **y** précédé d'une consonne : le **y** se change en **i**.

happ**y** → happ**i**ly

- Adjectifs terminés en **-le** : le **e** se change en **y**.

comfortab**le** → comfortab**ly**

1 Transforme ces adjectifs en adverbes.

1. strong: ....
2. easy: ....
3. comfortable: ....
4. dangerous: ....
5. heavy: ....
6. simple: ....
7. nice: ....
8. patient: ....
9. bad: ....
10. quick: ....

LES ADVERBES DE FRÉQUENCE
Often (*souvent*), **sometimes** (*quelquefois*), **always** (*toujours*), **never** (*jamais*), **usually** (*habituellement*) sont des adverbes de fréquence. Où se placent-ils ?
- Avant le verbe quand il est seul.

He **never** smokes. *Il ne fume jamais.*

- Toujours après **be.**

He is **always** late. *Il est toujours en retard.*

2 Replace l'adverbe dans la phrase.

1. I drink coffee. (*never*) ....
2. My English teacher is early. (*always*) ....
3. They go to the swimming-pool. (*often*) ....
4. My doctor is very patient. (*usually*) ....
5. His parents take the train. (*often*) ....

WELL / VERY MUCH

- **Well** (adverbe correspondant à l'adjectif **good**) = *bien*. **Very much** = *beaucoup*.
- Où se placent-ils ? Observe ces deux exemples.

  She speaks English **well**. *Elle parle bien anglais.*

  I like this book **very much**. *J'aime beaucoup ce livre.*

Well et **very much** sont des adverbes ; ils se placent après le complément, car un adverbe ne peut séparer un verbe de son complément.

3 Comment dirais-tu… ?

1. J'aime beaucoup cette voiture.
   ....
2. Mon cousin américain parle très bien le français.
   ....
3. Je regarde toujours la télévision le soir.
   ....
4. Nous allons souvent à l'école en bus.
   ....
5. Il attend le train patiemment.
   ....

4 Forme des phrases à l'aide de ces mots en désordre.

1. likes / mother / much / my / jazz / very
   ....
2. her / waiting / is / patiently / he / for / ?
   ....
3. president / slowly / the / speaks / English
   ....
4. speak / well / she / very / French / does / ?
   ....
5. my / often / early / gets / up / mother
   ....

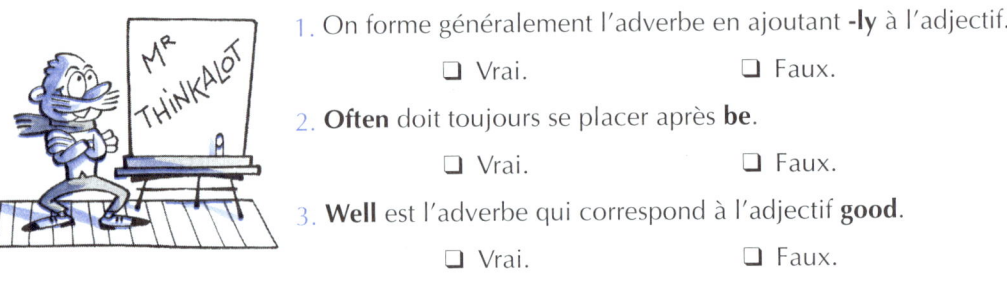

1. On forme généralement l'adverbe en ajoutant **-ly** à l'adjectif.
   ❏ Vrai.   ❏ Faux.
2. **Often** doit toujours se placer après **be**.
   ❏ Vrai.   ❏ Faux.
3. **Well** est l'adverbe qui correspond à l'adjectif **good**.
   ❏ Vrai.   ❏ Faux.

TROUVE DANS LA GRILLE LES NEUF ADVERBES SUIVANTS. LEQUEL FIGURE DEUX FOIS ? LES CINQ LETTRES RESTANTES, UNE FOIS MISES DANS LE BON ORDRE, TE DONNERONT LE MOT MYSTÉRIEUX.

O	F	T	E	N	S	O	E
S	O	M	E	T	I	M	E
U	S	U	A	L	L	Y	S
N	W	A	R	M	L	Y	W
E	A	L	W	A	Y	S	E
V	S	O	F	T	E	N	L
E	N	I C	E	L	Y	L
R	S	L	O	W	L	Y	H

THE MYSTERIOUS WORD IS : ☐☐☐☐☐

UNITÉ 10
Quelques indéfinis de quantité

Les indéfinis de quantité servent à exprimer une quantité sans la préciser.

MANY / MUCH / A LOT OF

Many, much, a lot of servent à exprimer l'idée d'une grande quantité.

- **Many** + dénombrable (ce qu'on peut compter).
  - Are there **many computers** in your school?
  - *Y a-t-il beaucoup d'ordinateurs dans ton école ?*

- **Much** + indénombrable (ce qu'on ne peut pas compter).
  - There isn't **much milk** in the bottle. *Il n'y a pas beaucoup de lait dans la bouteille.*

Many et **much** s'emploient surtout dans les phrases interrogatives et négatives.

- **A lot of** + dénombrable ou indénombrable.
  - I've got **a lot of friends**. *J'ai beaucoup d'amis.*
  - I've got **a lot of time**. *J'ai beaucoup de temps.*

1 Complète les phrases suivantes en utilisant many ou much.

1. I haven't got .... money.
2. Are there .... people in the street?
3. Have they got .... children?
4. There isn't .... water in the vase.
5. I can't eat .... eggs.

SOME / ANY

Some et **any** servent à exprimer une quantité non définie. Ils correspondent souvent à "du", "de la", "des". On les emploie devant les indénombrables (ce qu'on ne peut pas compter) et les dénombrables pluriel.

- Dans les phrases affirmatives : **some**.
  - There is **some** champagne in my glass. *Il y a du champagne dans mon verre.*
  - There are **some** letters on your table. *Il y a des lettres sur ta table.*

- Dans les phrases interrogatives : **any** ou **some.**
  - **any** quand on ne sait pas s'il y a ce que l'on demande.
    - Have you got **any** tea? *Avez-vous du thé ?*
    - Are there **any** eggs in the fridge? *Y a-t-il des œufs dans le frigo ?*
  - **some** quand on sait qu'il y a ce que l'on demande ou lorsqu'on fait une offre. On attend une réponse affirmative..
    - Can I have **some** bread, please? Of course.
    - *Est-ce que je peux avoir du pain, s'il te plaît ? Bien sûr.*

• Dans les phrases négatives : **any**.
On emploie **any** dans une phrase négative contenant **not**.
I do**n't** have **any** money. *Je n'ai pas d'argent.*
There are**n't any** letters for you. *Il n'y a pas de lettres pour vous.*

2 Complète les phrases suivantes en utilisant some ou any.

1. There are .... bicycles in the garage.
2. I haven't got .... brothers.
3. Is there .... milk in the fridge?
4. Take .... sandwiches for the picnic.
5. She's drinking .... beer.

3 Trouve les questions correspondant aux réponses données.

Exemple : Are there any sweets in the box? Yes, there are some sweets in the box.

1. .... ? Yes, there's some perfume in the bottle.
2. .... ? No, there aren't any children in the garden.
3. .... ? Yes, there is some bread.
4. .... ? No, there aren't any steaks.
5. .... ? Yes, there are some glasses on the table.

4 Regarde les dessins et réponds aux questions comme dans l'exemple suivant.

Exemple :
Are there any books on the table? No, there aren't any.
There are some cups.

1. Is there any butter in the fridge? ....
....

2. Are there any theatres in your street? ....
....

3. Are there any shoes in the box? ....
....

4. Is there any cake in the plate? ....
....

5. Are there any cars in the garage? ....
....

1. Pour dire qu'il y a beaucoup de livres, on utilisera :
   ❏ Many.   ❏ Much.
2. Pour dire qu'il y a beaucoup de sucre, on utilisera :
   ❏ Many.   ❏ Much.
3. Pour dire que tu as des lettres dans ton sac, tu emploieras :
   ❏ Any.   ❏ Some.

UNITÉ 11
Les prépositions

Les prépositions servent à introduire un complément, à situer les choses ou les personnes dans l'espace et le temps. Elles sont invariables.

LES PRINCIPALES PRÉPOSITIONS

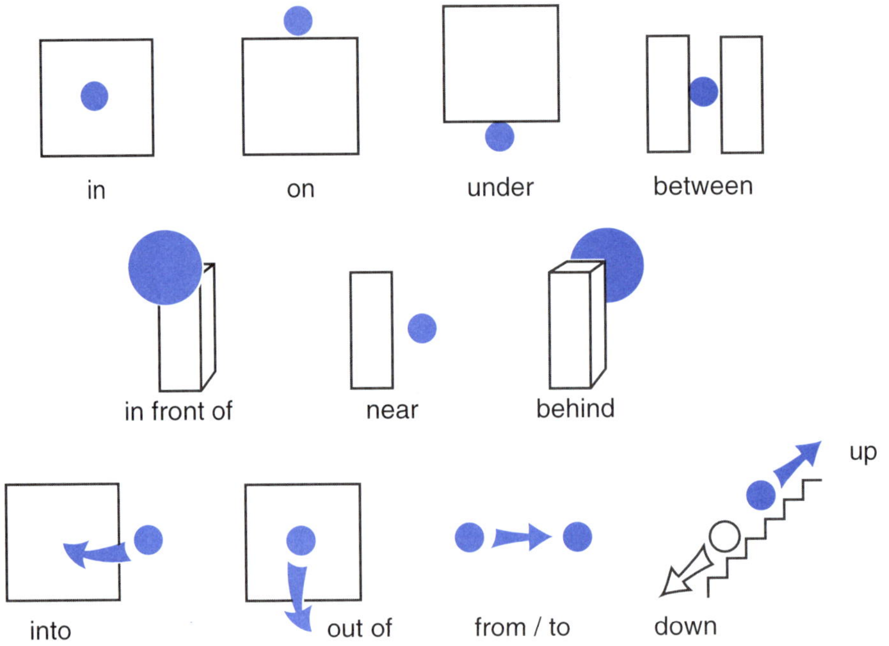

in   on   under   between

in front of   near   behind

into   out of   from / to   up   down

- **From** indique la provenance, le point de départ. **To** indique le point à rejoindre.
    They come **from** Tokyo. *Ils viennent de Tokyo.*
    I am going **to** the park. *Je vais au parc.*

- Ne confonds pas **at** et **to**. Compare ces deux phrases.

She is **at** the cinema. *Elle est au cinéma.*
(Point fixe, pas de déplacement.)

She is going **to** the cinema. *Elle va au cinéma.*
(Point à rejoindre. Déplacement.)

1 Réponds aux questions suivantes en utilisant la préposition qui convient.

1. Is he under the bike?
No, ...

2. Is he sitting on the bed?
No, ... chair.

3. Is the dog in front of the tree?
No, ...

4. Are they going down the mountain?
No, ...

5. Is the ladder under the door?
No, ... the window and the door.

2 Complète les phrases en utilisant des prépositions.

1. The children are .... the garden.
2. They are .... school.
3. The woman is sitting .... the chair.
4. Mary is going .... the circus.
5. They come .... New York.

3 Regarde les dessins et choisis la bonne réponse.

1. The hat is **on / in / behind** the man's head.

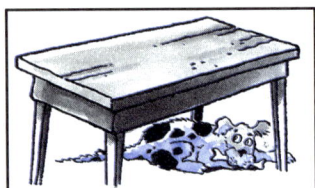

2. The dog is **on / in front of / under** the table.

3. The lamp is **behind / down / between** the sofa and the plant.

4. He's sleeping **under / in front of / in** his bed.

5. She's going **up / down / under** the stairs.

LISTEN TO, WAIT FOR, LOOK AT

Certains verbes construisent toujours leur complément avec une préposition.

Peter is listening **to** music. *Peter écoute de la musique.*
Mrs Black is waiting **for** her daughter. *Mrs Black attend sa fille.*
Philip is looking **at** a magazine. *Philip regarde un magazine.*

Attention ! À la forme interrogative, la préposition est rejetée à la fin, après le verbe.

What is Philip looking **at**? *Qu'est-ce que Philip regarde ?*

1. Les prépositions prennent la marque du pluriel.
   ❏ Vrai.   ❏ Faux.
2. La préposition **to** indique qu'il y a un déplacement, une destination.
   ❏ Vrai.   ❏ Faux.
3. Pour indiquer la provenance, on utilise :
   ❏ From.   ❏ Of.

THE PICTURE

Complète le dessin à l'aide des indications données.

THERE'S A BLUE CAR ON THE BRIDGE.

THE CAT'S IN THE TREE.

A WOMAN'S GOING UP THE LADDER.

A CHILD'S SLEEPING UNDER THE BRIDGE.

RICHARD'S PLAYING WITH A RACKET.

THREE CARS ARE PARKED NEAR THE TREE.

THERE'S A BOAT ON THE RIVER.

UNITÉ 12
Le présent de be

Be peut être un auxiliaire ou un verbe d'état. Il renseigne sur ce que l'on est.

LA FORME AFFIRMATIVE

Forme affirmative pleine	Forme affirmative contractée
I am	I'm
You are	You're
He, she, it is	He, she, it's
We are	We're
You are	You're
They are	They're

La forme affirmative peut être contractée. C'est surtout le cas à l'oral, dans une conversation.

1 **Complète en employant le verbe be. N'utilise pas de contractions.**

1. She .... English.
2. I .... from Canada.
3. He .... eleven.
4. They .... in the living-room.
5. You .... my friend.
6. We .... Italian.
7. It .... very late.

2 **Mets les phrases suivantes à la forme contractée.**
Remplace le sujet donné par le pronom personnel correspondant.

Exemple : Robert is in the street. → He's in the street.

1. Peter is in the bathroom. ....
2. Her friends are in the car. ....
3. My car is yellow. ....
4. Karen and Sally are at home. ....
5. My house is near the park. ....
6. Jane is in London. ....
7. Mary's pullover is red. ....

LA FORME INTERROGATIVE

Pour l'obtenir, on fait passer le verbe avant le sujet (inversion).

Forme interrogative pleine	
Am I?	Are we?
Are you?	Are you?
Is he, she, it?	Are they?

3 Les phrases suivantes sont-elles à la forme affirmative ou interrogative ? Coche la bonne case et ajoute la ponctuation.

	Forme affirmative	Forme interrogative
1. Who's that girl	❏	❏
2. That's a clock	❏	❏
3. How old are you	❏	❏
4. Where is my pullover	❏	❏
5. Peter's socks are white	❏	❏
6. What's your name	❏	❏
7. Is it your coat	❏	❏

4 Mets les phrases suivantes à la forme interrogative.

Exemple : It's a good book. → Is it a good book?

1. They're from Japan.

....

2. He's American.

....

3. The cat's under the tree.

....

4. That's Mr Black.

....

5. It's an armchair.

....

6. Mary's in the garden.

....

LA FORME NÉGATIVE

Pour l'obtenir, on ajoute la négation **not**, après **be**.

Forme négative pleine	Formes négatives contractées	
	1re forme	2e forme
I am not	I'm not	I'm not
You are not	You're not	You aren't
He, she, it is not	He, she, it's not	He, she, it isn't
We are not	We're not	We aren't
You are not	You're not	You aren't
They are not	They're not	They aren't

Les formes contractées sont surtout employées dans la conversation courante.

LES RÉPONSES BRÈVES

On répond rarement par **yes** ou **no** utilisés seuls. On reprend le sujet sous forme de pronom personnel et l'auxiliaire.

Is your mother at home? **Yes, she is.**

Is it an apple? **No, it isn't.**

Dans une réponse affirmative, on ne doit pas employer la forme contractée.

5   Donne des réponses brèves aux questions posées.

1. Are you English? No, ...
2. Is John at home? Yes, ...
3. Is your sister in her bedroom? Yes, ...
4. Are your parents here? No, ...
5. Is this your new car? Yes, ...

LES EXPRESSIONS AVEC BE

Plusieurs expressions ne contenant pas le verbe "être" en français se construisent avec **be** en anglais. Apprends à les reconnaître.

I**'m** cold, warm, hot.
J'ai froid, chaud, très chaud.
I**'m** hungry.
J'ai faim.
I**'m** thirsty.
J'ai soif.

I**'m** eleven.
J'ai onze ans.
I**'m** well (fine).
Je vais bien.
It**'s** fine today.
Il fait beau aujourd'hui.

CORRIGÉS

UNITÉ 1
Le nom

1. Dénombrables : chair, pen, dog, story, shoe, egg.
Indénombrables : butter, bread, time, milk, meat, salt.

2. 1. [z] 2. [iz] 3. [s] 4. [s] 5. [z] 6. [iz] 7. [s] 8. [iz]
9. [s] 10. [iz]

3. 1. The buses are coming.
2. Where are the blue socks?
3. The babies aren't sleeping.
4. Take your umbrellas.
5. Where are the boxes? Are they on the floor?
Trois mots forment leur pluriel en **es** : bus**es**, babi**es**, box**es**.

4. 1. The dogs aren't in the garden.
2. Are the children playing?
3. The postmen are bringing letters.
4. My brothers have got new rackets.
5. My feet are cold.

5. 1. The child isn't in the park.
2. Look at the man: he's playing football.
3. His shoe is all black.
4. Is the woman watching T.V.?
5. The knife is on the table.

Mr Thinkalot
1. Vrai 2. Faux 3. Vrai

One or two?
1. potatoes 2. matches 3. dresses 4. armchairs 5. women
6. buses 7. boxes 8. babies 9. umbrellas 10. sandwiches
11. children 12. postmen 13. men.
Le mot toujours au pluriel est : **trousers**.

UNITÉ 2
L'article

1. 1. a 2. an 3. an 4. a 5. ø 6. ø - ø

2. 1. Is he a doctor? No, he isn't. He's a dentist.
2. Is she an actress? No, she isn't. She's a nurse.
3. Are they engineers? No, they aren't. They're architects.
4. Is he a gardener? No, he isn't. He's a policeman.
5. Is she a princess? No, she isn't. She's a countess.

3. 1. the 2. the 3. the 4. the 5. the 6. the 7. the 8. the
9. the 10. the

4. 1. the 2. ø - ø 3. ø 4. ø - ø 5. the

Mr Thinkalot
1. Faux 2. Vrai 3. Faux

Don't forget !
1. an 2. ø 3. ø 4. the 5. ø 6. ø 7. ø 8. ø 9. the 10. the
11. a 12. ø

UNITÉ 3
L'adjectif qualificatif

1. 1. It's a new car.
2. It's a comfortable armchair.
3. It's a difficult exercise.
4. It's an expensive pen.
5. It's a big house.

2. 1. Her English teacher is nice and patient.
2. This is her new dress.
3. She is a very young doctor.
4. He is wearing a dirty pullover.
5. Is this an Italian restaurant?

3. 1. It's a big dog.
2. It's a dirty dress.
3. They're heavy boxes.
4. They're old houses.
5. She's a tall woman.

4. 1. young 2. cheap 3. small 4. long 5. bad

Mr Thinkalot
1. Vrai 2. Faux 3. Quand il est épithète.

On the contrary
1. small 2. cold 3. short 4. left 5. early 6. clean 7. new
8. bad
Le nom du pays est : **Scotland**.

UNITÉ 4
La comparaison

1. 1. My house is as big as Ted's house.
2. Her cousin is as tall as my brother.
3. Oliver is as hungry as Jim.
4. Tigers are as strong as lions.
5. Your shirt is as clean as my shirt.

2. 1. short: short**er** 2. fast: fast**er** 3. funny: funn**ier**
4. good: **better** 5. easy: easi**er** 6. happy: happ**ier** 7. clean: clean**er** 8. cheap: cheap**er** 9. rich: rich**er** 10. big: bigg**er**
11. heavy: heavi**er** 12. hot: hott**er** 13. small: small**er**.
The American speciality is the **hamburger**.

CORRIGÉS

3 1. The chocolate cake is better than the biscuits.
2. Betty is younger than Allison.
3. Her car is dirtier than Peter's car.
4. Your bag is heavier than my bag.
5. Your hair is longer than Jane's.
6. Tom is happier than Bob.
7. The Sahara desert is hotter than California.

4 1. This armchair is more comfortable than this chair.
2. Exercise 3 is more difficult than exercise 2.
3. This film is more interesting than this book.
4. Jessica is more polite than Julie.
5. Tigers are more dangerous than cats.
6. Mrs Bridge is more beautiful than Miss Smith.
7. My father is more careful than my uncle.

5 1. better than 2. easier than 3. bigger than 4. worse than 5. more elegant than

Mr Thinkalot

1. As 2. Vrai 3. Faux : c'est le comparatif irrégulier de **good**.

Older and heavier

1. Margaret, Dave and Jennifer. 2. Jennifer 3. Margaret 4. Jennifer and Dave 5. Jennifer 6. Margaret and Jonathan 7. Jonathan.

UNITÉ 5
Les pronoms personnels

1 1. they 2. she 3. he 4. they 5. we

2 1. him 2. them 3. us 4. me 5. them

3 1. her 2. they 3. us 4. it 5. him

4 1. I am waiting for them.
2. He is running after me.
3. Can you help us?
4. They can't buy a new car.
5. Give her a piece of cake.

Mr Thinkalot

1. Après le verbe 2. Vrai 3. Vrai

The balloons

1. Are we going to the circus? Yes, we are.
2. Is John smoking? No, he isn't.
3. Are the girls playing tennis? No, they aren't.
4. Can the boys go to the match? No, they can't.
5. Is it raining? Yes, it is.
6. Is Jane reading? Yes, she is.
7. Can you swim? Yes, I can.

UNITÉ 6
La possession

1 1. her 2. his 3. their 4. its 5. their

2 1. It's my mother's pen. It's her pen.
2. They're Philip's socks. They're his socks.
3. It's the Browns' cat. It's their cat.
4. They're Mrs Barret's glasses. They're her glasses.
5. It's Allison's newspaper. It's her newspaper.

3 1. No, it isn't. It's John's.
2. No, it isn't. It's Julie's.
3. No, it isn't. It's Oliver's.
4. No, it isn't. It's Sam's.
5. No, it isn't. It's my sister's.

4 1. Whose room is it? It's my parents'.
2. Whose eggs are they? They're Mr Miller's.
3. Whose rackets are they? They're the children's.
4. Whose dress is it? It's Diana's.
5. Whose baby is it? It's Susan's.

5 1. Whose bikes are they? They're their bikes.
2. Whose shoes are they? They're her shoes.
3. Whose ball is it? It's his ball.
4. Whose car is it? It's our car.
5. Whose breakfast is it? It's my breakfast.

6 1. He has got a present. 2. She has got a baby. 3. They have got cats. 4. He has got a ball. 5. She has got flowers.

Mr Thinkalot

1. Vrai 2. Whose? 3. Vrai.

Whose shoe is it?

Whose glasses are they? They're the postman's glasses.
Whose car is it? It's the taxi-driver's car.
Whose umbrella is it? It's Jennifer's umbrella.
Whose hat is it? It's the clown's hat.

UNITÉ 7
This / That

1 1. These are my books.
2. Those are my pens.

CORRIGÉS

3. These are your balls.
4. Those are my rackets.
5. These are my shoes.

2 1. What's this? It's a letter.
2. What's that? It's a plane.
3. What's that? It's a bird.
4. What's this? It's a shoe.
5. What's that? It's a chair.

3 1. That painting is expensive. 2. This pen is John's. 3. That rose is beautiful. 4. This cake is very good. 5. This exercise is easy.

Mr Thinkalot
1. Vrai 2. Vrai 3. Vrai

UNITÉ 8
Les mots interrogatifs

1 1. Where 2. When 3. What 4. Whose 5. Who

2 1. Who is in the garden?
2. Where is the transistor?
3. What is he eating?
4. Where are they?
5. Whose racket is it?
6. Who is coming with her?
7. When are they going to the circus?
8. Why is he washing his pullover?
9. Where is she sleeping?
10. What colour is his umbrella?

3 1. How are you? 2. How old is your sister? 3. How much money has he got? 4. How much is this pullover? 5. How many journalists are there…?

4 1. Whose dog is it?
2. Where's Sally?
3. What's he doing?
4. How old is Ken?
5. When is she going to the theatre?

5 1. What are you playing with?
2. What are you looking at?
3. What are you waiting for?
4. Where do you come from?
5. What are you listening to?

Mr Thinkalot
1. Vrai 2. Whose? 3. À la fin de la question

Cindy's diary
1. What 2. When 3. Who… with? 4. How much 5. What 6. Who 7. What time 8. Where 9. How many 10. When

UNITÉ 9
Les adverbes

1 1. strongly 2. easily 3. comfortably 4. dangerously 5. heavily 6. simply 7. nicely 8. patiently 9. badly 10. quickly

2 1. I never drink coffee. 2. My English teacher is always early. 3. They often go to the swimming-pool. 4. My doctor is usually very patient. 5. His parents often take the train.

3 1. I like this car very much.
2. My American cousin speaks French very well.
3. I always watch T.V. in the evening.
4. We often go to school by bus.
5. He's patiently waiting for the train. *ou* He is waiting for the train patiently.

4 1. My mother likes jazz very much.
2. Is he waiting for her patiently? *ou* Is he patiently waiting for her?
3. The president speaks English slowly.
4. Does she speak French very well?
5. My mother often gets up early.

Mr Thinkalot
1. Vrai 2. Vrai 3. Vrai

Never stupidly
L'adverbe **often** figure deux fois. Le mot mystérieux est : **shoes.**

UNITÉ 10
Quelques indéfinis de quantité

1 1. much 2. many 3. many 4. much 5. many

2 1. some 2. any 3. any 4. some 5. some

3 1. Is there any perfume in the bottle? 2. Are there any children in the garden? 3. Is there any bread? 4. Are there any steaks? 5. Are there any glasses on the table?

4 1. No, there isn't any. There are some eggs.
2. No, there aren't any. There are some cinemas.
3. No, there aren't any. There are some socks.
4. No, there isn't any. There are some apples.
5. No, there aren't any. There are some bicycles.

Mr Thinkalot
1. Many 2. Much 3. Some

CORRIGÉS

UNITÉ 11
Les prépositions

1 1. No, he's on the bike.
2. No, he's sitting on the chair.
3. No, he's behind the tree.
4. No, they're going up the mountain.
5. No, it's between the window and the door.

2 1. in 2. at 3. on 4. to 5. from

3 1. on 2. under 3. between 4. in 5. down

Mr Thinkalot
1. Faux 2. Vrai 3. From

The picture

Dessine une voiture bleue sur le pont, un chat dans l'arbre, une femme qui grimpe à l'échelle, un enfant qui dort sous le pont, une raquette entre les mains de Richard, trois voitures garées près de l'arbre, un bateau sur la rivière.

UNITÉ 12
Le présent de be

1 1. She is English. 2. I am from Canada. 3. He is eleven. 4. They are in the living-room. 5. You are my friend. 6. We are Italian. 7. It is very late.

2 1. He's in the bathroom.
2. They're in the car.
3. It's yellow.
4. They're at home.
5. It's near the park.
6. She's in London.
7. It's red.

3 1. Forme affirmative : phrases 2 et 5. Mettre un point.
2. Forme interrogative : phrases 1. 3. 4. 6. et 7. Mettre un point d'interrogation.

4 1. Are they from Japan?
2. Is he American?
3. Is the cat under the tree?
4. Is that Mr Black?
5. Is it an armchair?
6. Is Mary in the garden?

5 1. No, I'm not. 2. Yes, he is. 3. Yes, she is. 4. No, they aren't. 5. Yes, it is.

6 1. My mother is not thirsty.
2. He is ten (years old) today.

3. It is warm in the classroom.
4. Are you hungry?
5. How are you?

7 1. The boys are in the garden.
On ne peut pas utiliser **is** car le sujet est au pluriel.
2. I am from London.
On ne peut pas utiliser **is** car le sujet est à la première personne du singulier.
3. It is an English bus.
On ne peut pas utiliser **are** car le sujet est au singulier.
4. The sandwiches are in the kitchen.
On ne peut pas utiliser le mot **bread** car le verbe est au pluriel.

Mr Thinkalot
1. Faux 2. Vrai 3. Il faut barrer **has** car ce n'est pas une des formes de **be**.

Getting dressed
1C / 2D / 3E / 4F / 5A / 6B

UNITÉ 13
There is / there are

1 1. There are seven days… 2. There is a bird…
3. There is a lot of noise. 4. There are three rooms…

2 1. How many books are there on the table?
2. How many flowers are there in the vase?
3. How many shoes are there under the bed?
4. How many records are there near the lamp?
5. How many plants are there in the living-room?

3 **Are there?** permet d'interroger sur l'existence des choses. 1. Are they… 2. Are there… 3. Are there… 4. Are they… 5. Are there…

4 1. No, there isn't. 2. Yes, there are. 3. No, there isn't. 4. Yes, there is. 5. Yes, there are. 6. No, there aren't. 7. No, there isn't. 8. Yes, there is. 9. No, there isn't.

Mr Thinkalot
1. Faux 2. Faux 3. Faux

What's different?

In the second picture…
1. There is a shoe in the tree.
2. There are two balls under the chair.
3. There are five birds in the sky.
4. There is a dog behing the tree.
5. There are two hats under the tree.
6. There are no cats under the table.
7. There aren't any flowers under the chair.

4

CORRIGÉS

UNITÉ 14
Have got

1 1. I've got a walkman.
2. I've got two cats.
3. I've got a bird.
4. I've got a bike.
5. I've got a racket.
6. I've got a dog.

2 1. Helen 2. Peter and Jane 3. Mike 4. Sheila 5. Gary

3 1. Have you got a watch?
2. Have you got a bag?
3. Have you got a cake?
4. Have you got a racket?
5. Have you got a bike?
6. Have you got glasses?

4 1. Has Jane got a watch? No, she hasn't got one.
2. Have the Millers got a new car? No, they haven't got one.
3. Has Tom got a skateboard? No, he hasn't got one.
4. Have Peter and Sally got a dishwasher? No, they haven't got one.
5. Has Helen got a dog? No, she hasn't got one.
6. Have the children got a tennis ball? No, they haven't got one.

5 1. No, he hasn't.
2. Yes, they have.
3. Yes, I have.
4. No, she hasn't.
5. No, he hasn't.

6 1. How many stamps has she got?
2. How many cassettes have they got?
3. How many records has he got?
4. How many toys have they got?
5. How many postcards has he got?

7 1. No, she hasn't. She has got a car.
2. No, they haven't. They've got two girls.
3. No, she hasn't. She has got a fish.
4. No, they haven't. They've got a big dog.
5. No, he hasn't. He has got a shirt.

Mr Thinkalot

1. Faux 2. Vrai 3. Vrai

UNITÉ 15
Can - can't - must - mustn't

1 1. Kevin can play the piano. Cindy can't play the piano.
2. Kevin and Cindy can't speak French.
3. Kevin can't dance. Cindy can dance.
4. Kevin can make cakes. Cindy can't make cakes.

2 1. She mustn't sleep on the floor. She must sleep in her bed.
2. She mustn't brush her hair in the kitchen. She must brush her hair in the bathroom.
3. He mustn't cook in the bathroom. He must cook in the kitchen.
4. They mustn't do their homework in the hall. They must do it (their homework) in their room.
5. He mustn't put the bottles of milk on the T.V. set. He must put them (the bottles of milk) in the fridge.

3 1. What time must she get up?
2. What can I have after dinner?
3. Where must they go?
4. When can he go to the restaurant?
5. Who must they call?

4 1. Interdiction 2. Capacité 3. Capacité 4. Obligation
5. Impossibilité 6. Interdiction.

Mr Thinkalot

1. De l'infinitif sans **to** 2. Vrai 3. Vrai

Who's good for the job?

Miss Bridge: I can drive, I can play the piano, I can't speak Spanish, I can cook, I can't travel, I don't smoke.
Miss Harrington: I can travel, I can't cook, I can play the flute, I can speak Spanish, I smoke, I can't drive.
Mr Curtis: I can speak French, I can cook, I smoke, I can travel, I can play the guitar, I can't drive.
Mr Baker: I can drive, I can play the piano, I can speak Spanish, I can cook, I can travel, I don't smoke.
Mr Baker is good for the job.

UNITÉ 16
Les phrases réduites

1 1. isn't it?
2. aren't you?
3. aren't they?
4. is she?
5. isn't he?
6. are you?

2 1. is 2. are 3. isn't 4. aren't 5. isn't

3 1. Yes, I can. 2. No, they don't. 3. Yes, I am. (*ou* Yes, we are.) 4. Yes, she is. 5. No, he doesn't. 6. Yes, he can.
7. No, I haven't.

CORRIGÉS

Mr Thinkalot
1. Vrai 2. Contient une négation 3. Vrai

Pillow-talk
The complete sentences are:
1. Tom's your brother, isn't he?
2. Your car's red, isn't it?
3. His cousins aren't ready, are they?
4. It isn't cold, is it?
5. You are American, aren't you?
6. Your parents are at the theatre, aren't they?

A strange calculator
The message is : Lions never read magazines, do they? No, they don't.

UNITÉ 17
Le présent simple

1 Helen speaks English.
Glenn speaks English.
My sister speaks English.
Jenny speaks English.

Les autres combinaisons sont impossibles parce que le verbe a une terminaison en **-s** (3ᵉ personne du singulier). Donc le sujet ne peut être qu'au singulier.

2

	Auxiliaire	Sujet	Base verbale	Compléments
1.	Do	you	like	hamburgers?
2.	Does	your sister	play	tennis?
3.	Do	their children	speak	French?
4.	Does	he	take	the bus?
5.	Do	you	watch	T.V. every evening?

3 1. Yes, he does.
2. Yes, I do.
3. No, he doesn't.
4. No, they don't.
5. No, I don't.
6. Yes, they do.

4 Phrases à cocher : 2 - 5 - 7 - 10

5 1. Do they get up early? No, they don't get up early.
2. Does he drink a lot of milk? No, he doesn't drink a lot of milk.
3. Do they know the answer? No, they don't know the answer.
4. Does she sing very well? No, she doesn't sing very well.
5. Does the film begin at 3 o'clock? No, the film doesn't begin at 3 o'clock.

Mr Thinkalot
1. ... à la forme affirmative. 2. Faux 3. Vrai 4. Faux
5. ... d'une action habituelle

UNITÉ 18
Le présent progressif

1 1. They are buying… 2. She is drinking… 3. The little boy is falling. 4. We are eating… 5. My brother is listening… 6. Charles is going… 7. I am doing…

2 1. What are you doing? 2. What are you doing?
3. What are they doing? 4. What is he doing? 5. What is she doing?

3 1. What is Peter eating? 2. Who is Lucy phoning?
3. Where are the children going? 4. What are Bob and Sally making? 5. What is Shirley doing in her room?
6. What are they watching? 7. Who is playing with Philip?

4 1. Yes, they are.
2. Yes, he is.
3. No, I'm not.
4. No, it isn't.
5. Yes, he is.
6. No, they aren't.

5 1. Michael goes to the cinema every week.
2. The children are playing in the garden this afternoon.
3. We listen to the radio every morning.
4. Look! He's pushing the car.
5. They're coming for dinner this evening.

6 1. Do you understand?
2. Is Mary coming with us?
3. Are Peter and Jane going to the circus?
4. Do they take the bus every morning?
5. Are you writing a letter?
6. Is Dave making an omelette?
7. Do your parents buy fruit every day?

Non. Certaines phrases sont au présent simple, d'autres au présent progressif.
Avant de choisir l'auxiliaire, il faut voir si la base verbale a une terminaison en **-ing**.

7 1. Is she writing a letter?
2. Does he buy a lot of chocolates?
3. Is she sitting on the sofa?
4. Do they watch T.V. every day?
5. Are they going to a party?

Non, car certaines phrases sont au présent simple (→ auxiliaire **do**) et d'autres au présent progressif (→ auxiliaire **be**).

CORRIGÉS

Mr Thinkalot

1. Vrai 2. Faux 3. They go to England every year.

What are they doing?

1. It's seven o'clock. She's getting up.
2. It's a quarter past eight. She's going to school.
3. It's one o'clock. They're having lunch.
4. It's a quarter to seven. They're having dinner.
5. It's eight o'clock. They're watching T.V.
6. It's eleven o'clock. He's sleeping.

UNITÉ 19
Le prétérit simple

1 1. No, it wasn't. 2. Yes, they were. 3. Yes, he was. 4. Yes, he was. 5. No, I wasn't. (No, we weren't). 6. No, he / she wasn't.

2 1. liked 2. looked at 3. called 4. asked 5. were

3 1. Was she late?
2. Were they at home?
3. Did they watch T.V. yesterday evening?
4. Did she look at their photos?
5. Did they take the bus?

4 1. Fred didn't call a taxi.
2. He wasn't very angry.
3. My father didn't arrive before dinner.
4. Betty didn't like the film.
5. We weren't tired.

5 1. Yes, they did. 2. No, I didn't. 3. No, I wasn't. 4. Yes, he (she) did. 5. Yes, it was.

Mr Thinkalot

1. À la forme affirmative 2. Vrai 3. She is very surprised.

Darts

1. Susan was at school.
2. I played tennis last Wednesday.
3. My brothers watched television yesterday evening.
4. John went to school with Mary.
5. Was he late for school?
6. Antony gave me a book for my birthday.
7. We ate a lot of chocolate after dinner.
8. Were you at the concert yesterday?
Les trois fléchettes qui n'ont pas servi sont **took**, **entered** et **arrived**.
The drink is : **tea**.

UNITÉ 20
L'expression du futur

1 1. She is going to phone Sue.
2. She is going to write to her grandma.
3. She is going to buy an umbrella.
4. She is going to make a cake.
5. She is going to go to the supermarket.

2 1. Are your parents going to invite their friends? No, they aren't.
2. Is Michael going to call Laura? No, he isn't.
3. Is your sister going to do her homework? No, she isn't.
4. Are you going to take a taxi? No, I'm not.
5. Is John going to make a cake? No, he isn't.

3 1. He's giving a concert tonight.
He's going to give a concert tonight.
2. I'm going on holiday in August.
I'm going to go on holiday in August.
3. They're having a party next Saturday.
They're going to have a party next Saturday.

4 1. No, I'm not. 2. No, he isn't. 3. Yes, they are. 4. Yes, she is. 5. Yes, I am (we are).

Mr Thinkalot

1. Are they going to visit the museum? (futur avec **going to**)
He is inviting his friends next Saturday. (présent progressif + **next Saturday**) 2. Vrai

A day in his life

C'est **Bob**.

UNITÉ 21
Les phrases impératives

1 1. Don't play with your pencil.
2. Don't sleep in your armchair.
3. Don't put your shoes on your bed.
4. Don't brush your hair in the kitchen.
5. Don't play football in the living-room.

2 1. Don't drink in class.
2. Shut the window.
3. Don't forget your homework.
4. Don't eat chewing-gum.
5. Don't speak with your friend.

3 1. Listen to me. 2. Look at the pictures. 3. Open the door. 4. Sing with me. 5. Call your sister.

CORRIGÉS

Do's and don'ts

Les ordres à barrer sont : 1, 3, 4, 5, 8, 9, 11, 12, 13.

UNITÉ 22
L'heure

• As-tu bien observé?
1. Vrai 2. It's ten. It's ten o'clock. 3. Past 4. To

 1. It's ten past nine. 2. It's twenty-five to seven. 3. It's half past eleven. 4. It's five to five. 5. It's a quarter to eight. 6. It's twenty past three.

2. 1.  2.  3.
4.  5.  6.

UNITÉ 23
Les nombres et la date

1 1. thirteen
2. twenty-nine
3. forty-five
4. sixty-four
5. ninety-three

2 1. 278
2. 425
3. 500
4. 792
5. 805

3 1st: first
2nd: second
3rd: third
9th: ninth
12th: twelfth
20th: twentieth
85th: eighty-fifth

4 Le mot mystérieux est : **number.**

5 1. 1998
2. 1869
3. 1972
4. 1785
5. 1523

6 1. nineteen forty-six
2. eighteen twenty-four
3. fifteen fifteen
4. nineteen ninety-seven
5. sixteen fifty-eight

6. Comment dirais-tu que … ?

1. Ta mère n'a pas soif.

....

2. Il a dix ans aujourd'hui.

....

3. Il fait chaud dans la classe.

....

Comment demanderais-tu à un ami … ?

4. S'il a faim.

....

5. Comment il va.

....

7. Remets les mots dans le bon ordre pour faire des phrases. Il y a un mot en trop dans chaque liste. Explique pourquoi on ne peut pas l'utiliser.

1. boys / in / is / the / garden / are / the

....

2. I / from / am / is / London

....

3. it / an / are / is / English / bus

....

4. the / sandwiches / bread / are / kitchen / the / in

....

1. Dans une phrase interrogative, le sujet est placé avant le verbe.

❏ Vrai.   ❏ Faux.

2. Dans une phrase négative, l'ordre des mots est le suivant : sujet + auxiliaire **be** + négation.

❏ Vrai.   ❏ Faux.

3. Barre l'intrus.

Is - am - are - has.

getting dressed

AIDE CES PERSONNAGES À S'HABILLER EN CHOISISSANT LE BON CHAPEAU ET LA BONNE ÉCHARPE. RETROUVE LA RÉPONSE BRÈVE CORRESPONDANT À CHAQUE QUESTION.

1. IS ELTON JOHN A CLOWN?
2. ARE YOU AMERICAN?
3. ARE WE LATE?
4. IS LUCY A PIANIST?
5. ARE YOUR PARENTS AT HOME?
6. IS IT A NEW BOOK?

A. NO, THEY AREN'T.
B. YES, IT IS.
C. NO, HE ISN'T.
D. YES, I AM.
E. YES, WE ARE.
F. NO, SHE ISN'T.

1. . . . .
2. . . . .
3. . . . .
4. . . . .
5. . . . .
6. . . . .

UNITÉ 13
There is / There are

Ces expressions permettent de parler de l'existence ou de l'absence d'une chose ou d'une personne, de parler de ce qu'il y a. Elles peuvent s'employer aux formes affirmative, interrogative et négative.

LA FORME AFFIRMATIVE

- Compare ces deux phrases.

There is a tree in the garden. **There are** five trees in the garden.
Il y a un arbre dans le jardin. *Il y a cinq arbres dans le jardin.*

There is est suivi d'un nom singulier. **There are** est suivi d'un nom pluriel. **Be** s'accorde donc avec le nom qui suit.

- On peut contracter **there is**: **there's**. On ne peut pas contracter **there are**.
  There's a tree in the garden. **There are** trees in the garden.

- Si le premier mot d'une liste de mots est au singulier, on emploie **there is**.
  There is a dog, three cats and two birds.
  Il y a un chien, trois chats et deux oiseaux.

1 **Complète avec** there is **ou** there are.

1. .... seven days in a week.
2. .... a bird in the classroom.
3. .... a lot of noise.
4. .... three rooms in my house.

LES FORMES INTERROGATIVE ET NÉGATIVE

À la forme interrogative, on fait l'inversion: on emploie **is there?** ou **are there?**
À la forme négative, on emploie **there isn't** ou **there aren't**.

   Is there a letter for me? *Est-ce qu'il y a une lettre pour moi ?*
   There isn't any bread. *Il n'y a pas de pain.*

2 **Un bruit bizarre t'a empêché d'entendre le nombre contenu dans chacune de ces phrases. Pose la question qui te permettra de le connaître.**

Exemple : There are 🔊 cakes in the kitchen. → How many cakes are there in the kitchen?

1. There are 🔊 books on the table. ....
2. There are 🔊 flowers in the vase. ....
3. There are 🔊 shoes under the bed. ....
4. There are 🔊 records near the lamp. ....
5. There are 🔊 plants in the living-room. ....

3   **Quel groupe de mots permet d'interroger sur l'existence des choses ?**

❏ Are there?   ❏ Are they?

Complète les phrases suivantes en utilisant Are there? **ou** Are they?

1. .... playing in the garden?
2. .... lots of caramels in the box?
3. .... any apples in the kitchen?
4. .... painting their room?
5. .... theatres in your town?

LES RÉPONSES BRÈVES AVEC THERE IS, THERE ARE

Is there a plant in your room? **Yes, there is.**
Are there many carrots? **Yes, there are.**
Is there a western on television? **No, there isn't.**
Are there cartoons? **No there aren't.**
Dans une réponse affirmative, on ne doit pas employer la forme contractée.

---

4   **Regarde le dessin et donne des réponses brèves aux questions.**

1. Is there a lamp behind the chair? ....
2. Are there flowers in the vase? ....
3. Is there an armchair near the door? ....
4. Is there a poster on the wall? ....
5. Are there books on the desk? ....
6. Are there any records on the desk? ....
7. Is there a woman in the room? ....
8. Is there a boy on the bed? ....
9. Is there a plant under the window? ....

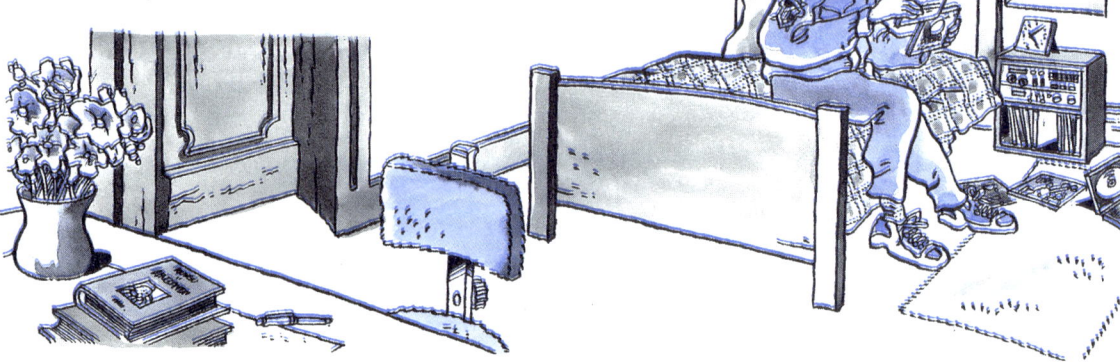

1. L'expression "il y a" est invariable en français. Il en est de même pour son équivalent anglais.

❑ Vrai.   ❑ Faux.

2. On doit utiliser **there are** si l'on veut dire qu'il y a un lapin et deux tortues dans le jardin.

❑ Vrai.   ❑ Faux.

3. **They are** et **there are** ont le même sens.

❑ Vrai.   ❑ Faux.

WHAT'S DIFFERENT?

OBSERVE BIEN CES DEUX DESSINS, ILS SONT PRESQUE SEMBLABLES. COMPLÈTE LES PHRASES SUIVANTES POUR PARLER DES DIFFÉRENCES QUE TU AS REMARQUÉES.

IN THE SECOND PICTURE
1. .... A SHOE IN THE ....
2. .... TWO BALLS UNDER THE ....
3. .... FIVE .... IN THE SKY.
4. .... A .... BEHIND THE TREE.
5. .... TWO HATS UNDER THE ....
6. .... NO .... UNDER THE TABLE.
7. .... ANY FLOWERS UNDER THE ....

UNITÉ 14
Have got

Have got sert à parler de ce que l'on possède. Cette forme exprime également les liens de parenté.
Have se conjugue et got reste invariable.

LA FORME AFFIRMATIVE

Forme affirmative pleine	Forme affirmative contractée
I have got	I've got
You have got	You've got
He, she, it has got	He, she, it's got
We have got	We've got
You have got	You've got
They have got	They've got

1 Que dit Brian pour parler de ce qu'il possède ?

1. ....
2. ....
3. ....
4. ....
5. ....
6. ....

2 Regarde l'arbre généalogique et trouve de qui il s'agit.

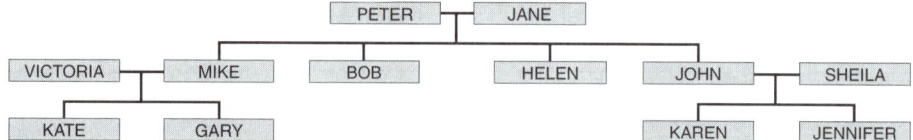

1. She has got three brothers. Her name is ....
2. They have got four children. Their names are ....
3. He has got two children. His wife's name is Victoria. His name is ....
4. She has got two daughters. Her name is ....
5. He has got two uncles. His name is ....

LA FORME INTERROGATIVE

Pour la construire, on fait l'inversion :

> Have I got? Have we got?
> Have you got? Have you got?
> Has he, she, it got? Have they got?

3 Brian veut maintenant savoir ce que possède son ami Dave. Quelles questions lui pose-t-il ?

1. ....
2. ....
3. ....
4. ....
5. ....
6. ....

LA FORME NÉGATIVE

Pour l'obtenir, on ajoute la négation **not** après l'auxiliaire **have**.

Forme affirmative pleine	Forme affirmative contractée
I have not got	I haven't got
You have not got	You haven't got
He, she, it has not got	He, she, it hasn't got
We have not got	We haven't got
You have not got	You haven't got
They have not got	They haven't got

Le présent se forme avec **have** ou sa forme contractée à toutes les personnes, sauf à la 3ᵉ personne du singulier où l'on emploie **has** ou sa forme contractée.
Les formes contractées sont plus souvent utilisées que les formes pleines.

A la 3ᵉ personne du singulier, ne confonds pas les formes contractées de **be** et **have**.
She**'s got** a cat. *Elle a un chat.*   She**'s** a singer. *Elle est chanteuse.*
La forme contractée de **be** n'est pas suivie de **got**.

4   Pose des questions et réponds par une phrase négative.

Exemple : Michael / a motorbike / Has Michael got a motorbike? No, he hasn't got one.

1. Jane / a watch ....
2. the Millers / a new car ....
3. Tom / a skateboard ....
4. Peter and Sally / a dishwasher ....
5. Helen / a dog ....
6. the children / a tennis ball ....

LES RÉPONSES BRÈVES

On répond rarement par **yes** ou **no** utilisés seuls. On reprend le sujet sous forme de pronom personnel et l'auxiliaire.
Have your parents got a piano? **Yes, they have.**
Has your sister got a car? **No, she hasn't.**

5   Donne des réponses brèves.

1. Has Tim got a new car? No, ...
2. Have the boys got tennis rackets? Yes, ...
3. Have you got a lot of books? Yes, ...
4. Has Jane got a red dress? No, ...
5. Has he got brown trousers? No, ...

6   Pose des questions en commençant par how many.

Exemple : I have got a lot of books. How many books have you got?

1. My sister has got a lot of stamps.   .... ?
2. His parents have got a lot of cassettes.   .... ?
3. My brother has got a lot of records.   .... ?
4. Their children have got a lot of toys.   .... ?
5. His uncle has got a lot of postcards.   .... ?

7 Regarde les dessins et réponds aux questions.

Exemple : Has John got a cat? No, he hasn't. He has got a dog.

1. Has Susan got a bicycle?
   ....

2. Have they got a boy?
   ....

3. Has she got a rabbit?
   ....

4. Have the Millers got a small dog?
   ....

5. Has Brian got a pullover?
   ....

1. **Have got** a la même forme à toutes les personnes.
   ❏ Vrai.   ❏ Faux.
2. **Got** est invariable.
   ❏ Vrai.   ❏ Faux.
3. À la forme interrogative, **have** se place avant le sujet.
   ❏ Vrai.   ❏ Faux.

UNITÉ 15
Can - can't - must - mustn't

Can et must sont des auxiliaires modaux. Les auxiliaires modaux modifient le sens des verbes qu'ils accompagnent. Ils expriment des nuances très variées : capacité, obligation, interdiction…

RÈGLES GÉNÉRALES
- Ils sont suivis d'un verbe à l'infinitif sans **to**.
- Ils ont la même forme à toutes les personnes (donc pas de **s** à la 3ᵉ personne du singulier du présent).
- Ils se conjuguent sans **do** aux formes interrogative et négative.

À la forme interrogative, on fait passer l'auxiliaire modal devant le sujet.

Observe bien à gauche les exemples, à droite le sens des différents modaux.

CAN - CAN'T

He **can** carry the big suitcase. *Il peut porter la grosse valise.* **Can** you speak English? *Savez-vous parler anglais ?*	Capacité physique ou intellectuelle (traduit quelquefois par "savoir").
Can I go out tonight? *Est-ce que je peux sortir ce soir ?*	Permission.
Can you give me a pen? *Peux-tu me donner un stylo ?*	Demande polie.
What **can** you see? *Que voyez-vous ?*	Capacité (devant les verbes de perception : **see**, **hear**…).

I **can't** call you tonight. *Je ne peux pas t'appeler ce soir.*	Incapacité, impossibilité.
You **can't** play in the morning. *Tu ne peux pas jouer le matin.*	Interdiction.
I **can't** hear you! *Je ne t'entends pas !*	Incapacité (devant les verbes de perception : **see**, **hear**…).

1 Regarde les réponses de Kevin et Cindy aux questions suivantes et rédige des phrases.

	Kevin	Cindy
Can you play the piano?	Yes	No
Can you speak French?	No	No
Can you dance?	No	Yes
Can you make cakes?	Yes	No

1. Kevin can play the piano. Cindy ....
2. ....
3. ....
4. ....

MUST - MUSTN'T

- You **must** go to bed. *Tu dois aller au lit.*   • Obligation.
- You **mustn't** smoke. *Tu ne dois pas fumer.*   • Interdiction.

2 Réagis aux phrases suivantes en utilisant **mustn't** et **must** comme dans l'exemple ci-dessous.

Exemple : John's playing football in his bedroom. → He mustn't play football in his bedroom. He must play football in the garden.

1. Susan is sleeping on the floor.

   ....

2. She is brushing her hair in the kitchen.

   ....

3. Bill is cooking in the bathroom.

   ....

4. The children are doing their homework in the hall.

   ....

5. Ben is putting the bottles of milk on the T.V. set.

   ....

3 Un bruit bizarre t'a empêché d'entendre une partie de la phrase. Pose la question qui te permettra de comprendre de quoi on parle.

1. Susan must get up at half .

....?

2. You can have after dinner.

....?

3. They must go to .

....?

4. Peter can go to the restaurant on .

....?

5. They must call Mr .

....?

4 Quelles sont les notions exprimées par les phrases suivantes ?

	Interdiction	Capacité	Impossibilité	Obligation
1. You can't smoke.	❏	❏	❏	❏
2. He can speak Italian.	❏	❏	❏	❏
3. He can run very fast.	❏	❏	❏	❏
4. They must do their homework.	❏	❏	❏	❏
5. I can't come today.	❏	❏	❏	❏
6. You mustn't drive too fast.	❏	❏	❏	❏

1. Un auxiliaire modal est toujours suivi :

❏ De l'infinitif sans **to.**   ❏ De la base verbale + **-ing.**

2. Les auxiliaires modaux sont invariables.

❏ Vrai.   ❏ Faux.

3. À la forme interrogative, les auxiliaires modaux se placent avant le sujet.

❏ Vrai.   ❏ Faux.

UNITÉ 16
Les phrases réduites

Les phrases réduites sont très souvent utlisées en anglais. Elles servent à demander confirmation, à marquer l'étonnement, la surprise…

LES QUESTION-TAGS

● Les **question-tags** sont de petites questions qui viennent en fin de phrase et qui servent généralement à demander confirmation. Elles correspondent au français "n'est-ce pas ?", mais sont employées plus couramment.

● Observe ces phrases.

It's delicious, **isn't it**? *C'est délicieux, n'est-ce pas ?*
↑ ↑
1ʳᵉ partie affirmative Tag négatif.

My parents aren't late, **are they**? *Mes parents ne sont pas en retard, n'est-ce pas ?*
↑ ↑
1ʳᵉ partie négative   Le tag ne contient pas de négation.

● Remarque bien :
• Le sujet du **question-tag** est toujours un pronom personnel.
• L'auxiliaire est toujours placé avant le sujet.
• Un **question-tag** est toujours précédé d'une virgule et suivi d'un point d'interrogation.

● Le **question-tag** n'est généralement pas une vraie question : on n'attend pas de réponse. Dans ce cas, l'intonation n'est pas celle de la forme interrogative : on emploie une intonation descendante.

---

1 Complète les phrases suivantes à l'aide du question-tag qui convient.

1. The fish is good, ……………… ?
2. You're cold, ……………… ?
3. The Millers are late, ……………… ?
4. Karen isn't pleased, ……………… ?
5. That boy's stupid, ……………… ?
6. You aren't ready, ……………… ?

2 À l'aide du question-tag, retrouve l'auxiliaire manquant de la première partie de la phrase (mets-le à la forme négative si nécessaire).

1. This armchair ……………… comfortable, isn't it?
2. His trousers ……………… blue, aren't they?
3. It ……………… funny, is it?
4. You ……………… late, are you?
5. Kate's dog ……………… big, is he?

LES RÉPONSES BRÈVES (OU RÉPONSES COURTES)

● On répond rarement en anglais par **yes** ou **no** employés seuls. On utilise généralement la formule :
- **Yes +,** + pronom personnel sujet + auxiliaire.
- **No +,** + pronom personnel sujet + auxiliaire + négation.

  Do you speak French? **Yes, I do.**
  Are the children sleeping? **No, they aren't.**
  Can you play the violin? **Yes, I can.**
  Have they got a dog? **No, they haven't.**

● À la forme affirmative, on ne doit pas employer la forme contractée.

  Are you tired? **Yes, I am**. *Es-tu fatigué ? Oui.*

3. Donne des réponses brèves.

1. Can you swim? Yes, ...
2. Do they like coffee? No, ...
3. Are you pleased? Yes, ...
4. Is she reading a book? Yes, ...
5. Does he play cricket? No, ...
6. Can he play Monopoly? Yes, ...
7. Have you got a computer? No, ...

1. Dans un **question-tag**, l'auxiliaire est toujours placé avant le sujet.
   ❏ Vrai.   ❏ Faux.

2. Quand la première partie de la phrase est affirmative, le **question-tag** :
   ❏ Est affirmatif aussi.   ❏ Contient une négation.

3. Dans une réponse brève, le sujet est toujours repris sous forme de pronom personnel.
   ❏ Vrai.   ❏ Faux.

THE COMPLETE SENTENCES ARE:

1. ....
2. ....
3. ....
4. ....
5. ....
6. ....

UNITÉ 17
Le présent simple

Il existe deux formes de présent : le présent simple et le présent progressif (ou présent en **be** + **ing**). Pour parler des actions habituelles, des vérités, des faits permanents, on utilise le présent simple.

LA FORME AFFIRMATIVE

I work	We work
You work	You work
He, she, it works	They work

- À la forme affirmative, on utilise la base verbale à toutes les personnes.
- La 3ᵉ personne du singulier se termine toujours par un **s**. Cette terminaison doit s'entendre et se prononce [s] ou [z].

1 Quels sujets peut-on relier à la forme verbale ci-dessous ?
Écris autant de phrases correctes que possible en utilisant le verbe et les sujets donnés.

Mr and Mrs Todd

Jenny   **speaks English**   Helen

My sister   Glenn   My parents

The boys

....
....
....
....
....

Certaines combinaisons sont impossibles. Pourquoi ?
....
....

LES FORMES INTERROGATIVE ET NÉGATIVE

Forme interrogative	Forme négative
Do I work?	I don't work
Do you work?	You don't work
Does he, she, it work?	He, she, it doesn't work
Do we work?	We don't work
Do you work?	You don't work
Do they work?	They don't work

• Les formes interrogative et négative se construisent à l'aide de l'auxiliaire **do**. **Do** devient **does** à la 3e personne du singulier.

• Attention à l'ordre des mots.

Auxiliaire	Sujet	Base verbale
Do	you	smoke?
Does	he	drive?

Sujet	Auxiliaire + négation	Base verbale
I	don't	smoke.
He	doesn't	drive.

• Attention : la base verbale ne prend pas de **s**. C'est **does** qui porte la marque de la 3e personne du singulier.

2 Remets dans l'ordre les mots suivants pour construire des questions correctes.

1. you / do / hamburgers / like / ?
2. your / tennis / does / play / sister / ?
3. their / speak / French / do / children / ?
4. take / does / he / the / bus / ?
5. T.V. / evening / do / watch / you / every / ?

Auxiliaire	Sujet	Base verbale	Complément (s)
1.	....	....	....
2.	....	....	....
3.	....	....	....
4.	....	....	....
5.	....	....	....

LES RÉPONSES BRÈVES

Pour former la réponse brève, on reprend le sujet sous forme de pronom personnel et l'auxiliaire.

Does Mary play the piano? Yes, **she does**.
Do your parents often go to the cinema? No, **they don't**.
Does Albert play football? No, **he doesn't**.
Do you like chocolate? Yes, **I do**!

3 Trouve la réponse brève correspondant à chacune de ces phrases.

1. Does your brother like cheese? Yes, ...
2. Do you play squash? Yes, ...
3. Does Peter often wear jeans? No, ...
4. Do your parents want to sleep? No, ...
5. Do you help your sister? No, ...
6. Do your friends read a lot? Yes, ...

L'EMPLOI DU PRÉSENT SIMPLE

Le présent simple sert à exprimer des actions habituelles, répétées, des vérités, des faits permanents.

John **takes** the bus at eight. *John prend l'autobus à huit heures*. (action habituelle)
The sun **rises** in the east. *Le soleil se lève à l'est*. (vérité permanente)

4 Coche les phrases qui parlent d'une action habituelle.

1. ❏ Helen is playing cards.
2. ❏ Gary tidies his room every day.
3. ❏ She's phoning her friend.
4. ❏ They're listening to the radio.
5. ❏ We never watch horror films.
6. ❏ The children are in their room.
7. ❏ Kevin plays football on Sundays.
8. ❏ Sandy is sleeping.
9. ❏ It's very late.
10. ❏ Maria's parents always speak Italian with their children.

5 **Mets les phrases suivantes à la forme interrogative, puis négative.**

1. They get up early.
2. He drinks a lot of milk.
3. They know the answer.
4. She sings very well.
5. The film begins at 3 o'clock.

Forme interrogative	Forme négative
1. Do they ....?	No, ...
2. ....?	No, ...
3. ....?	No, ...
4. ....?	No, ...
5. ....?	No, ...

1. L'auxiliaire **do** n'apparaît pas :
   ❏ À la forme affirmative.
   ❏ À la forme négative.
   ❏ À la forme interrogative.

2. Les verbes conjugués au présent simple prennent une terminaison en **-s** au pluriel.
   ❏ Vrai.   ❏ Faux.

3. **Do** devient **does** à la 3ᵉ personne du singulier.
   ❏ Vrai.   ❏ Faux.

4. On construit la forme négative en ajoutant la négation **not** à la base verbale.
   ❏ Vrai.   ❏ Faux.

5. On utilise le présent simple pour parler :
   ❏ D'une action habituelle.
   ❏ D'une action en train de se faire.

A STRANGE CALCULATOR

REGARDE LA CALCULATRICE ET DÉCOUVRE LE MESSAGE EN FAISANT LES ADDITIONS ET LES SOUSTRACTIONS.

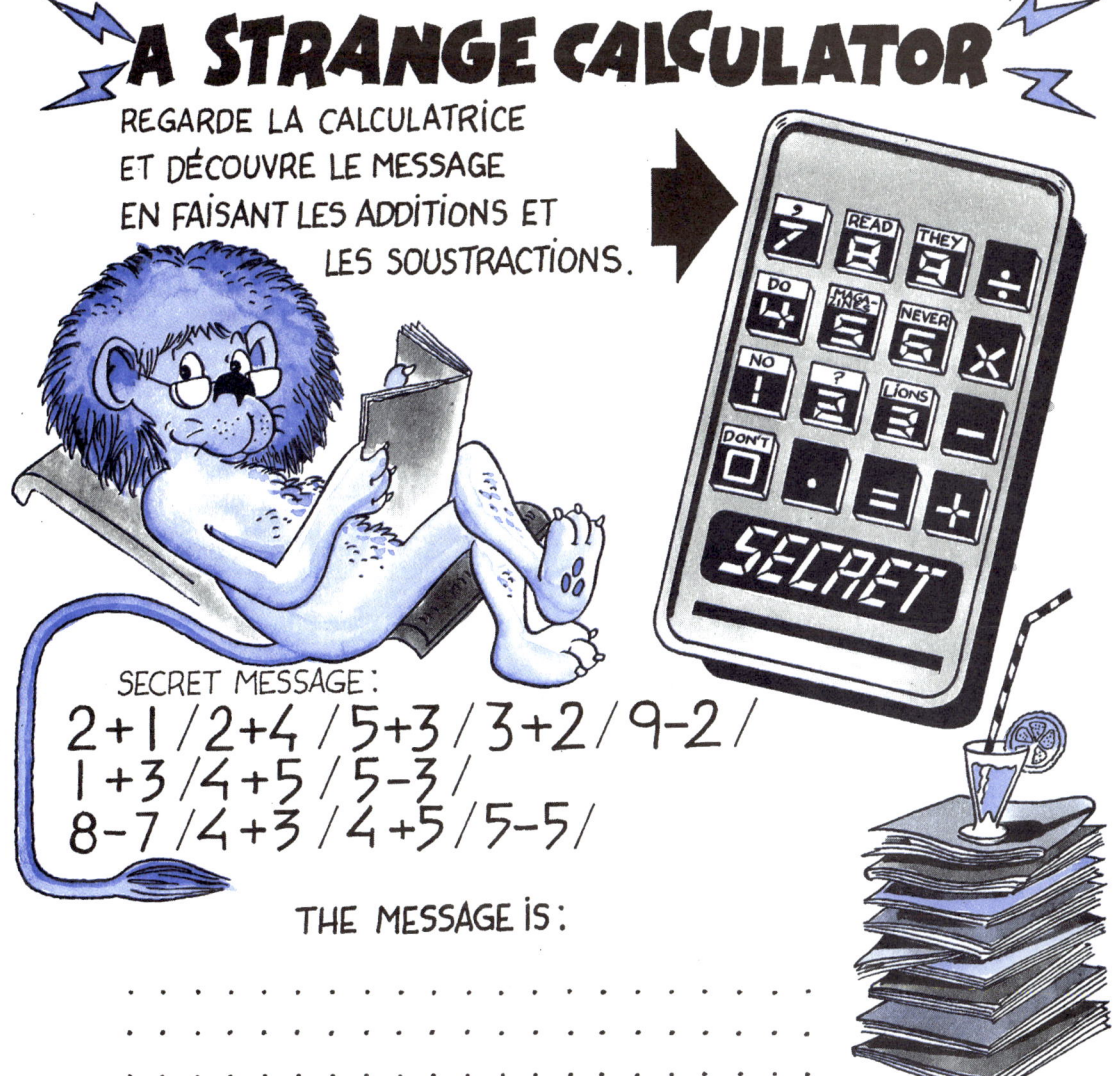

SECRET MESSAGE :
2+1 / 2+4 / 5+3 / 3+2 / 9-2 /
1+3 / 4+5 / 5-3 /
8-7 / 4+3 / 4+5 / 5-5 /

THE MESSAGE IS :

. . . .
. . . .
. . . .

UNITÉ 18
Le présent progressif

Pour parler de l'action qui se déroule en ce moment, on emploie le présent progressif (que l'on appelle également présent continu ou présent **be** + **ing**).

LA FORME AFFIRMATIVE

I am working	We are working
You are working	You are working
He, she, it is working	They are working

Une phrase au présent progressif contient toujours :
– le sujet,
– l'auxiliaire **be** conjugué au présent,
– la base verbale terminée par **-ing**.

Sujet	**Auxiliaire** be	**Base verbale + -ing**	**Complément**
He	is	eating	an apple.

1 Complète les phrases en utilisant le bon auxiliaire et la terminaison verbale pour obtenir des phrases au présent progressif.

1. They .... buy... ice-creams.
2. She .... drink... an orange-juice.
3. The little boy .... fall... .
4. We .... eat... toast and marmalade.
5. My brother .... listen... to jazz.
6. Charles .... go... to his piano lesson.
7. I .... do... my homework.

LA FORME INTERROGATIVE

Am I working?	Are we working?
Are you working?	Are you working?
Is he, she, it working?	Are they working?

Pour obtenir la forme interrogative, il suffit de faire l'inversion : l'auxiliaire passe avant le sujet.

Auxiliaire be	**Sujet**	**Base verbale + -ing**
Are	they	playing?

2 Retrouve les questions qui ont provoqué les réponses suivantes.

Exemple : What are you doing? I'm swimming.

1. ....?
I am watching a cartoon.

2. ....?
We are speaking.

3. ....?
They are playing golf.

4. ....?
He is drinking.

5. ....?
She is looking at a photo.

3 Un bruit bizarre t'a empêché d'entendre une partie de la phrase. Pose la question qui te permettra de comprendre de quoi on parle.

1. Peter is eating a .
....

2. Lucy is phoning her .
....

3. The children are going to .
....

4. Bob and Sally are making a .
....

5. Shirley is in her room.
....

6. They are watching a .
....

7. is playing with Philip.
....

LA FORME NÉGATIVE

I am not working	We aren't working
You aren't working	You aren't working
He, she, it isn't working	They aren't working

Sujet	Auxiliaire be + négation	Base verbale + -ing
Peter	isn't	sleeping.

LES RÉPONSES BRÈVES

On reprend le sujet sous forme de pronom personnel et l'auxiliaire **be**.

Are you working? **Yes, I am**.

Is your mother watching T.V.? **No, she isn't**.

4 Trouve la réponse brève qui correspond à chaque question.

1. Are the children working? Yes, ...
2. Is Matthew listening to records? Yes, ...
3. Are you going to the stadium? No, ...
4. Is it raining? No, ...
5. Is Philip washing his pullover? Yes, ...
6. Are the boys sitting on the bed? No, ...

L'EMPLOI DU PRÉSENT PROGRESSIF

Le présent progressif s'emploie pour parler des actions qui se déroulent en ce moment.

What **is** he **doing**? He**'s singing**.   *Que fait-il ? Il chante.*

5 Construis les phrases suivantes au présent simple ou progressif.

Exemple : John *(get up)* early today. John is getting up early today.
Peter *(make)* a cake every Sunday. Peter makes a cake every Sunday.

1. Michael (**go**) to the cinema every week.

....

2. The children (**play**) in the garden this afternoon.

....

3. We (**listen**) to the radio every morning.

....

4. Look ! He (**push**) the car.

....

5. They (**come**) for dinner this evening.

....

6 Complète les questions suivantes en utilisant un auxiliaire.

1. .... you understand?
2. .... Mary coming with us?
3. .... Peter and Jane going to the circus?
4. .... they take the bus every morning?
5. .... you writing a letter?
6. .... Dave making an omelette?
7. .... your parents buy fruit every day?

Les phrases que tu as complétées sont-elles toutes au même temps ?

....

Qu'as-tu observé avant de choisir le bon auxiliaire ?

....

7 Mets les phrases suivantes à la forme interrogative comme dans l'exemple donné. N'oublie pas de toujours commencer par un auxiliaire.

Exemple : Stephen is going to the zoo. → Is he going to the zoo?

1. Helen is writing a letter. ....
2. Bob buys a lot of chocolates. ....
3. Karen is sitting on the sofa. ....
4. Jane and Kate watch T.V. every day. ....
5. The Browns are going to a party. ....

As-tu toujours utilisé le même auxiliaire ? ....
Pourquoi ? ....
....

1. Dans une question au présent progressif, l'ordre des mots est : auxiliaire + sujet + base verbale + **-ing**

   ❏ Vrai.   ❏ Faux.

2. On utilise l'auxiliaire **do** pour construire la forme interrogative du présent progressif.

   ❏ Vrai.   ❏ Faux.

3. Quelle est la phrase qui ne parle pas d'une action en train de se faire ?

   ❏ She is reading a magazine.
   ❏ They go to England every year.

What are they doing?

RELIE LES DESSINS AUX HORLOGES. UTILISE LES VERBES POUR CONSTRUIRE DES PHRASES AU PRÉSENT PROGRESSIF.

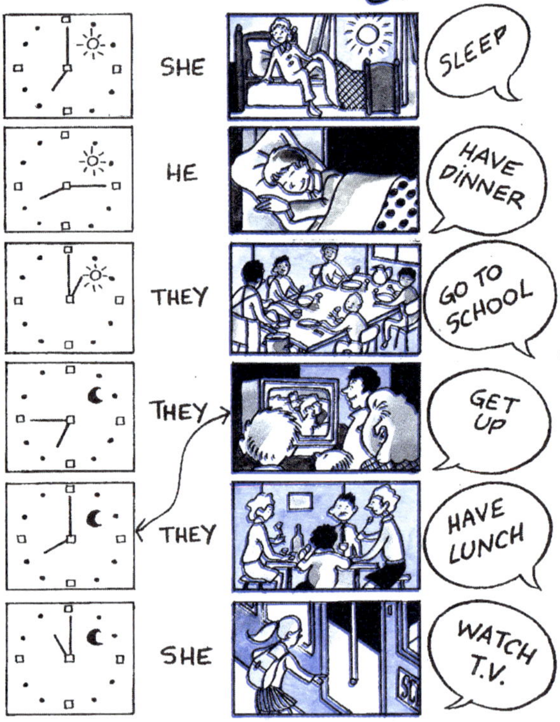

1 ▶ ....
2 ▶ ....
3 ▶ ....
4 ▶ ....
5 ▶ IT'S 8 O'CLOCK: THEY'RE WATCHING T.V.
6 ▶ ....

UNITÉ 19
Le prétérit simple

Le prétérit simple est un temps du passé. Tu pourras l'utiliser pour parler d'événements passés, de ton enfance, de ce que tu as fait hier…

PRÉTÉRIT DE BE
Be est le seul verbe qui a deux formes au prétérit : **was** et **were**.

LA FORME AFFIRMATIVE

I was	We were
You were	You were
He, she, it was	They were

I **was** in London last week. *J'étais à Londres la semaine dernière.*

LES FORMES INTERROGATIVE ET NÉGATIVE

- Pour construire la forme interrogative, il suffit de faire passer l'auxiliaire avant le sujet.
  Were they at home yesterday? *Étaient-ils à la maison hier ?*

- Pour construire la forrme négative, on met la négation **not** après l'auxiliaire.
  He **wasn't** very pleased. *Il n'était pas très content.*

LES RÉPONSES BRÈVES
On utilise le pronom personnel sujet et l'auxiliaire.
Was she at school? **Yes, she was**.
Was it a good film? **No, it wasn't**.

---

1 Donne des réponses brèves aux questions suivantes.

1. Was the window open? No, ...
2. Were your parents at home? Yes, ...
3. Was Tom late for school? Yes, ...
4. Was the dog in the garden? Yes, ...
5. Were you on holidays? No, ...
6. Was the teacher angry? No, ...

PRÉTÉRIT DES VERBES RÉGULIERS
LA FORME AFFIRMATIVE

- À la forme affirmative, le prétérit des verbes réguliers se termine par **-ed** à toutes les personnes.

    work → work**ed**   love → lov**ed**

- La terminaison doit s'entendre. On prononce [t] ou [d] selon la voyelle ou la consonne qui précède. Il faut choisir la prononciation la plus facile, celle qui vient le plus naturellement.
Le nombre de syllabes reste le même que celui de la base verbale.

    look → look**ed** [t] = une syllabe.
    disappear → disappear**ed** [d] = trois syllabes.

On prononce [id] lorsque la base verbale se termine par le son [t] ou [d] : sinon la terminaison **-ed** ne s'entendrait pas.

    want → want**ed** [id]   decide → decid**ed** [id]

Dans ce cas, le prétérit comporte une syllabe de plus que la base verbale :

    repeat = deux syllabes   repeat**ed** = trois syllabes.

---

2 **Mets les verbes donnés au prétérit.**

1. My parents .... the presents. *(like)*
2. Jimmy .... the pictures. *(look at)*
3. I .... my parents yesterday. *(call)*
4. The students .... a lot of questions. *(ask)*
5. We .... in the kitchen. *(be)*

LES FORMES INTERROGATIVE ET NÉGATIVE

Elles se construisent à l'aide de l'auxiliaire **did**. **Did** est le prétérit de **do**.

Forme interrogative

Auxiliaire	Sujet	Base verbale	Compléments
Did	you	see	John yesterday?

Forme négative

Auxiliaire	Sujet	Base verbale	Complément
I	didn't	like	the film

On utilise à toutes les personnes **did** + le verbe à l'infinitif sans **to**, car c'est **did** qui est la marque du prétérit.

3 Mets les phrases suivantes à la forme interrogative.

1. She was late. ....
2. My parents were at home. ....
3. They watched T.V. yesterday evening. ....
4. Sue looked at their photos. ....
5. My cousins took the bus. ....

4 Mets les phrases suivantes à la forme négative.

1. Fred called a taxi. ....
2. He was very angry. ....
3. My father arrived before dinner. ....
4. Betty liked the film. ....
5. We were tired. ....

PRÉTÉRIT DES VERBES IRRÉGULIERS

Un certain nombre de verbes ne forment pas leur prétérit en **-ed**. Ils ont une forme irrégulière qu'il faut apprendre par cœur. Cette forme est la même à toutes les personnes.

buy → I **bought**, you **bought**…   see → I **saw**, you **saw**…
eat → I **ate**, you **ate**…   take → I **took**, you **took**…
go → I **went**, you **went** … (liste p. 86)

RÉPONSES BRÈVES

Pour former une réponse brève, on utilise le pronom personnel sujet et l'auxiliaire **did**.
Did you phone him yesterday? **Yes, I did.**
Did she play tennis yesterday? **No, she didn't.**

5 Donne des réponses brèves aux questions suivantes.

1. Did your sisters bring their rackets? Yes, ...
2. Did you like this book? No, ...
3. Were you tired yesterday? No, ...
4. Did the teacher talk to you? Yes, ...
5. Was the window open? Yes, ...

1. L'auxiliaire **did** ne doit pas être utilisé à la forme :

   ❏ Affirmative.
   ❏ Négative.
   ❏ Interrogative.

2. Aux formes interrogative et négative, le passé est indiqué par **did** et le verbe reste à l'infinitif sans **to**.

   ❏ Vrai.   ❏ Faux.

3. Quelle est la phrase qui ne contient pas une idée de passé ?

   ❏ I didn't visit the tower.   ❏ He worked a lot yesterday.
   ❏ She is very surprised.   ❏ They were in San Francisco.

darts

OÙ DOIVENT SE PLANTER LES FLÉCHETTES POUR COMPLÉTER LES PHRASES ? ÉCRIS LES VERBES MANQUANTS AU BON ENDROIT. TROIS FLÉCHETTES NE SERVIRONT PAS. LEURS PREMIÈRES LETTRES, PLACÉES DANS LE BON ORDRE, TE DONNERONT LE NOM D'UNE BOISSON.

Fléchettes : ATE, ENTERED, WERE, WATCHED, WAS, WAS, GAVE, PLAYED, ARRIVED, TOOK, WENT

1. SUSAN ... AT SCHOOL.
2. I ... TENNIS LAST WEDNESDAY.
3. MY BROTHERS ... TELEVISION YESTERDAY EVENING.
4. JOHN ... TO SCHOOL WITH MARY.
5. ... HE LATE FOR SCHOOL ?
6. ANTONY ... ME A BOOK FOR MY BIRTHDAY.
7. WE ... A LOT OF CHOCOLATE AFTER DINNER.
8. ... YOU AT THE CONCERT YESTERDAY ?

THE DRINK IS : . . .

UNITÉ 20
L'expression du futur

Pour parler de l'avenir, on peut utiliser plusieurs constructions différentes.

BE GOING TO + BASE VERBALE

- On peut exprimer le futur en utilisant **be going to** + base verbale. Dans cette expression, l'auxiliaire **be** se conjugue au présent. **Going to** et la base verbale restent invariables.
  I'm **going to buy** a motorbike. *Je vais acheter une moto.*
  She's **going to paint** her room. *Elle va peindre sa chambre.*

- Forme interrogative = auxiliaire + sujet + **going to** + base verbale.
  Are you going to phone him? *Vas-tu l'appeler ?*

- Forme négative = sujet + auxiliaire **be** + **not** + **going to** + base verbale.
  He isn't going to sing. *Il ne va pas chanter.*

- L'expression **be going to** permet d'exprimer l'intention, la résolution, de prédire un événement.

---

1 Regarde la liste rédigée par Pamela et dis ce qu'elle va faire.

1. phone Sue ....
2. write to grandma ....
3. buy an umbrella ....
4. make a cake ....
5. go to the supermarket ....

2 Utilise les éléments donnés pour construire une question et donner une réponse négative.

Exemple : you / play tennis → Are you going to play tennis? No, I'm not.

1. your parents / invite their friends
   ....
2. Michael / call Laura
   ....
3. your sister / do her homework
   ....
4. you / take a taxi
   ....
5. John / make a cake
   ....

LE PRÉSENT PROGRESSIF

On peut aussi exprimer le futur en utilisant le présent progressif lorsque le sujet est un être animé et que la phrase contient un complément de sens futur.

He's leaving **tomorrow**. *Il part demain.*
They're coming **at five**. *Ils viennent à cinq heures.*

3 À partir des éléments donnés, construis des phrases de sens futur. Utilise deux constructions différentes.

Exemple : I / take the plane / tomorrow. → I'm taking the plane tomorrow. I'm going to take the plane tomorrow.

1. he / give a concert / tonight
....
....

2. I / go on holiday / in August
....
....

3. they / have a party / next Saturday
....
....

LES RÉPONSES BRÈVES

On utilise le pronom personnel sujet et l'auxiliaire **be**.

Is she going to buy a new car? **Yes, she is.**
Are they going to decorate their room? **No, they aren't.**
Is he taking the plane tomorrow? **Yes, he is.**

4 Donne des réponses brèves.

1. Are you going to take the train? No, ...
2. Is Tim going to buy a new car? No, ...
3. Are they going to have a party next Saturday? Yes, ...
4. Is Shirley going to visit Paris? Yes, ...
5. Are you going to see them at six? Yes, ...

1. Quelles sont les phrases qui contiennent une idée de futur ?

   ❏ She is going to the cinema.
   ❏ Are they going to visit the museum?
   ❏ Does she often watch TV?
   ❏ He is inviting his friends next Sunday.

2. Dans une phrase au futur avec **be going to**, la base verbale est invariable.

   ❏ Vrai.   ❏ Faux.

A DAY IN HIS LIFE

REGARDE CES PAGES D'AGENDA.
UN SEUL PERSONNAGE VA FAIRE
TOUTES LES ACTIVITÉS MENTIONNÉES.
LEQUEL ?

TIM'S DIARY — MONDAY, 15th
SUPERMARKET
12.30: HENRY
TENNIS WITH MARK
DENTIST
PUB
9: HAMLET

BOB'S DIARY — MONDAY, 15th
SUPERMARKET
12: SUSIE
2: WIMBLEDON
WRITE TO UNCLE PAUL
PUB
8: ROMEO AND JULIET

JOHN'S DIARY — MONDAY 15TH
10: HOSPITAL
SUPERMARKET
LUNCH WITH Mr BROWN
TELEGRAM TO Mrs GEORGE
PUB
8.30: JAZZ FESTIVAL

▶ HE'S GOING TO BUY SOME MILK, SOME SOAP AND SOME MEAT.
▶ HE'S GOING TO HAVE A BEER AT THE PUB.
▶ HE'S GOING TO GO TO THE THEATRE.
▶ HE'S GOING TO SEE A TENNIS MATCH.
▶ HE'S GOING TO HAVE LUNCH WITH HIS GIRLFRIEND.
▶ HE'S GOING TO SEND A LETTER.

UNITÉ 21
Les phrases impératives

L'emploi de l'impératif anglais est proche de celui du français. Il sert à donner des ordres, des conseils, à interdire…

FORME AFFIRMATIVE

Pour obtenir les phrases impératives à la 2ᵉ personne, on emploie la base verbale dans des phrases sans sujet.

Give me the key. *Donne-moi la clé.*
Look at the road. *Regarde la route.*
Open the door. *Ouvre la porte.*

FORME NÉGATIVE

À la forme négative, la base verbale est précédée de **don't**.

Don't wake him up. *Ne le réveillez pas.*
Don't worry. *Ne t'inquiète pas.*
Don't smoke here. *Ne fumez pas ici.*

---

1 Utilise l'impératif pour demander aux personnes de ne pas faire ce qu'elles font.

Exemple : He's eating his sandwich now. → Don't eat your sandwich now.

1. He is playing with his pencil.
   ....

2. She is sleeping in her armchair.
   ....

3. He is putting his shoes on his bed.
   ....

4. He is brushing his hair in the kitchen.
   ....

5. She is playing football in the living-room.
   ....

2 Ton professeur parle : complète les phrases en utilisant les verbes donnés. Emploie la forme négative si cela est nécessaire.

1. .... in class. *(drink)*

2. .... the window. It's cold. *(shut)*

3. .... your homework. *(forget)*

4. .... chewing-gum. *(eat)*

5. .... with your friend. *(speak)*

3 Utilise des phrases à l'impératif pour demander à quelqu'un de :

1. t'écouter : ....

2. regarder les images : ....

3. ouvrir la porte : ....

4. chanter avec toi : ....

5. appeler sa sœur : ....

do's and don'ts

BARRE LES ORDRES QUI NE CORRESPONDENT PAS À CE QUE LES PARENTS PEUVENT DIRE À LEURS ENFANTS.

1. WALK ON THE ROOF!
2. GO TO BED!
3. DON'T DO YOUR EXERCISES!
4. PUT THE WET DOG IN YOUR BED!
5. PUT THE CAT INTO THE BATH!
6. BRUSH YOUR TEETH!
7. WASH YOUR HANDS!
8. PUT YOUR BIKE IN THE KITCHEN!
9. OPEN THE FRIDGE EVERY 5 MINUTES!
10. DON'T WATCH T.V. TOO LATE!
11. EAT CHOCOLATE FOR DINNER!
12. PUT YOUR DIRTY SOCKS ON THE TABLE!
13. DON'T TAKE OFF YOUR COAT!
14. TAKE YOUR KEY!

UNITÉ 22
L'heure

• Regarde bien ces pendules.

It's five o'clock. / It's five.   It's ten past five.   It's a quarter past five.

It's twenty past five.   It's half past five.   It's twenty to six.   It's ten to six.

• As-tu bien observé ?
1. En anglais, on exprime les minutes avant les heures.
   ❏ Vrai.   ❏ Faux.
2. Pour dire qu'il est dix heures juste, on peut dire :
   ❏ It's ten.   ❏ It's ten o'clock.   ❏ It's about ten.
3. Si l'on veut dire qu'il est dix heures vingt-cinq, on emploie :
   ❏ To.   ❏ Past.
4. Si l'on veut dire qu'il est onze heures moins dix, on emploie :
   ❏ To.   ❏ Past.

1 Quelle heure est-il ? Inscris l'heure sous chaque pendule.

1. ....   2. ....

3. ....   4. ....

5. ....   6. ....

2 Regarde l'heure indiquée sous chaque pendule et dessine les aiguilles.

1. It's a quarter past six.

2. It's two to two.

3. It's five to ten.

4. It's half past twelve.

5. It's ten past one.

6. It's three o'clock.

UNITÉ 23
Les nombres et la date

Il existe deux types de nombres : les cardinaux et les ordinaux. Les nombres cardinaux sont généralement employés comme déterminants. Ils représentent une quantité précise. Les nombres ordinaux permettent de classer, de donner un rang (premier, deuxième, troisième…).

LES CARDINAUX

1	one	12	twelve	30	thirty
2	two	13	thirteen	31	thirty-one
3	three	14	fourteen	32	thirty-two…
4	four	15	fifteen	40	forty
5	five	16	sixteen	50	fifty
6	six	17	seventeen	60	sixty
7	seven	18	eighteen	70	seventy
8	eight	19	nineteen	80	eighty
9	nine	20	twenty	90	ninety
10	ten	21	twenty-one		
11	eleven	22	twenty-two…		

1 Écris en toutes lettres.

13 : ....

29 : ....

45 : ....

64 : ....

93 : ....

100	a / one hundred		
101	a / one hundred and one	200	two hundred
110	a / one hundred and ten	295	two hundred and ninety-five

Retiens bien :
- Hundred ne prend pas de s.
- Hundred est suivi de and.

He has got **two hundred and twenty-five** stamps. *Il a deux cent vingt-cinq timbres.*

2 Écris en chiffres.

1. two hundred and seventy-eight: ....

2. four hundred and twenty-five: ....

3. five hundred: ....

4. seven hundred and ninety-two: ....

5. eight hundred and five: ....

LES ORDINAUX

1st	first		11th	eleventh
2nd	second		12th	twelfth
3rd	third		13th	thirteenth
4th	fourth		20th	twentieth
5th	fifth		21st	twenty-first
6th	sixth		30th	thirtieth
7th	seventh		31st	thirty-first
8th	eighth		32nd	thirty-second
9th	ninth		100th	hundredth
10th	tenth			

Attention à la prononciation des noms de rois : Elizabeth **the Second** (Elizabeth II), Richard **the Third** (Richard III), Henry **the Eighth** (Henry VIII).

---

3 **Fais correspondre chaque nombre ordinal avec son écriture en lettres.**

1st	eighty-fifth
2nd	twelfth
3rd	twentieth
9th	first
12th	third
20th	second
85th	ninth

4 **Trouve le mot mystérieux en répondant aux questions. Inscris dans la grille la lettre correspondante.**

1. What's the second letter of the word **animal**? ☐
2. What's the first letter of the word **umbrella**? ☐
3. What's the third letter of the word **game**? ☐
4. What's the first letter of the word **bed**? ☐
5. What's the fifth letter of the word **garden**? ☐
6. What's the eighth letter of the word **November**? ☐

U23

LA DATE

Pour lire une année, on dit d'abord les deux premiers chiffres, puis les deux derniers : 1996 = nineteen ninety-six.
On écrit : July 14th, 1789 ou 14th July 1789 (moins courant).
On dit : July, the fourteenth seventeen eighty-nine ou the fourteenth of July seventeen eighty-nine.

5 Écris les dates suivantes en chiffres.

1. nineteen ninety-eight: ....
2. eighteen sixty-nine: ....
3. nineteen seventy-two: ....
4. seventeen eighty-five: ....
5. fifteen twenty-three: ....

6 Écris en toutes lettres les dates suivantes.

1. 1946 : ....
2. 1824 : ....
3. 1515 : ....
4. 1997 : ....
5. 1658 : ....

- **Verbes irréguliers**

- **Index**

VERBES IRRÉGULIERS

Base verbale	Prétérit	Participe passé	
B			
be	was, were	been	*être*
begin	began	begun	*commencer*
buy	bought	bought	*acheter*
C			
come	came	come	*venir*
cut	cut	cut	*couper*
D			
do	did	done	*faire*
drink	drank	drunk	*boire*
E			
eat	ate	eaten	*manger*
F			
fall	fell	fallen	*tomber*
find	found	found	*trouver*
G			
get	got	got	*devenir, obtenir*
give	gave	given	*donner*
go	went	gone	*aller*
H			
have	had	had	*avoir*
hear	heard	heard	*entendre*
K			
keep	kept	kept	*garder*
know	knew	known	*savoir, connaître*

Base verbale	Prétérit	Participe passé	
M			
make	made	made	*faire, fabriquer*
P			
put	put	put	*mettre*
R			
read	read	read	*lire*
run	ran	run	*courir*
S			
say	said	said	*dire*
see	saw	seen	*voir*
sing	sang	sung	*chanter*
sit	sat	sat	*s'asseoir*
sleep	slept	slept	*dormir*
speak	spoke	spoken	*parler*
stand	stood	stood	*être debout*
T			
take	took	taken	*prendre*
tell	told	told	*dire*
think	thought	thought	*penser*
U			
understand	understood	understood	*comprendre*
W			
wear	wore	worn	*porter*
write	wrote	written	*écrire*

INDEX

A
a	8
adjectifs qualificatifs	11
adverbes	32
adverbes de fréquence	32
a lot of	35
an	8
any	35, 36
article défini	9
article indéfini	8
as … as	14
auxiliaires	42, 50
auxiliaires modaux	54

B
be	42
be going to	75

C
can	54
can't	54
cas possessif	22
comparatif	14

D
date	84
démonstratifs	26
dénombrables	4
déterminants (articles)	8
do	62
did	72

F
futur (expression du)	75

G
génitif	22

H
have got	23, 50
heure	80
how?	29
how many?	29
how much?	29
how old?	29

I
impératives (phrases)	78
indénombrables	4
indéfinis	35
interrogatifs (mots)	28

M
many	35
modaux (auxiliaires)	54
more	16
much	35
must	55
mustn't	55

N
nom	4
nombres	82

P
phrases réduites	58
pluriels irréguliers	5
possessifs	21
possession (notion de)	21, 50
prépositions	38
prépositions (place des)	30, 40
présent progressif (ou présent continu)	66, 76
présent simple	42, 61
prétérit simple	71
pronoms personnels	18

Q
quantité (notion de)	35
question-tags	58

R
réponses brèves (ou réponses courtes)	59

S
some	35

T
than	14, 16
that	26
the	9
there is	47
there are	47
these	26
this	26
those	26

V
verbes irréguliers	73, 86
very much	33

W
was, were	71
well	33
what?	28
when?	28
where?	28
who?	28
whose?	22, 28
why?	28

Imprimé en France par l'Imprimerie Hérissey - 27000 Évreux - Dépôt légal : 10469 - Janvier 1998 - Nº d'impression : 79056